born again
and again

born again
and again

*surprising gifts
of a fundamentalist childhood*

■ ■ ■ ■ ■ ■ ■ ■

by Jon M. Sweeney

PARACLETE PRESS
BREWSTER, MASSACHUSETTS

2005 First Printing

ISBN 1-55725-431-1

All Scripture quotations are taken from the *King James Version* of
the Bible. Portions of this book appeared previously in *Sacred
Journey* and on www.explorefaith.org.

Author's note:
In order to protect the privacy of other people, some details of
chronology, names, and places have been changed slightly.

Library of Congress Cataloging-in-Publication Data

Sweeney, Jon M., 1967–
  Born again and again : surprising gifts of a fundamentalist
  childhood / by Jon M. Sweeney.
    p. cm.
  Includes bibliographical references.
  ISBN 1-55725-431-1
  1. Sweeney, Jon M. 1967– 2. Christian biography—United States.
3. Fundamentalists—United States—Biography. I. Title. Born
again and again. II Title.
BR1725.S885A3 2005
277.3'0825'092—dc22   2005010375

Published by Paraclete Press
Brewster, Massachusetts
www.paracletepress.com

10 9 8 7 6 5 4 3 2 1

Printed in the United States of America

For my kids, Sarah-Maria and Joseph.
One day you'll read this,
and we'll talk about it.

contents

■ ■ ■ ■ ■ ■ ■ introduction

Somewhere in the Zohar, the classic text of Jewish mysticism, it says, "The stories in the Torah couldn't be about what they say they're about because we could write better stories." I suspect that the same is true of the stories in our lives. When we look back, what we see as a simple narrative of what happened, or a single conversation, may actually be elements of something much larger, a bigger story. We play parts that we don't even know we play in other people's lives. A story of mine may actually turn out to intersect with a story of yours, and the narrative of your life may be a piece of the larger fabric that joins to my life, too.

A phrase written by Alexander Solzhenitsyn, the Russian writer who survived the Gulag, has always stuck with me. Trying desperately to remember his awful experiences under torture and isolation in that Siberian camp, he reflected that memory is like "a hackneyed dotted line." I may not know just exactly what my own stories mean, but this is my attempt, at least, to put them out there in an effort to understand them. These traces of the huge narrative of which I am a part are my way of walking the path that is mine to walk. I want to say these stories out loud, so to speak, in these pages in the hope that they might make some sense to me and so that they might spark something inside of you, the reader as well. That big narrative engulfs you, too. How are your paths leading from it, out of it, toward it?

What religious stories are inside of you, bubbling beneath the surface of your public self? I have gone out of my way not to tell these things in the past. Long ago, I deliberately dropped my first college off my résumé. For more than a decade, I intentionally avoided mention of much of my childhood faith in casual conversation with people I did not trust completely. But I understand now that my early religious experiences were essential to the formation of who I am and who I will become, and that even though I am no longer there—spiritually, physically, maybe emotionally—I am grateful for the journey and for what I learned on the way.

There are many surprising gifts of fundamentalist faith in my life. They are introduced throughout the pages that follow: God and life matter; we all need saving again and again; rebirth is the experience and optimism of forgiveness; we ought to love Scripture and study it; protest is necessary; older friends add value and wisdom to our lives; and, we all must own our faith and say it aloud.

If you are fundamentalist or evangelical (or *neo-evangelical*—if you can keep up with the distinctions!), you will likely recognize some of my experiences as similar to your own. But just as likely, you may disagree with how I have interpreted many of them. If so, stay in the dialogue with me, as our stories intersect. Meanwhile, if you are mainline Protestant, or Catholic, or Orthodox— and you grew up in one of those traditions—my religious experiences may be foreign to you, but you may be drawn through this book to recognize value in aspects of fundamentalism, as I do.

The chapters that follow are reflections on growing up in the American suburbs in the 1970s and 1980s in a distinctive brand of Christianity. Part One opens with the day that I knelt and asked Jesus to "come into my heart" (the most important event in the life of a born-again Christian) when I was five. It explains the wonder of a child raised to understand God as an intimate friend and explores the ways in which my family and two grandfathers, in particular, both conservative Baptist preachers for fifty years, influenced my own understanding and aspirations. In the first few chapters, I try to describe as accurately as I am able the spiritual feelings and ideas of a child living under the constant watch of God's eyes.

The chapter titles in Part Two are each taken from a phrase in the Nicene Creed—language that evokes more mystery than elicits explanation. Part Two follows my path through the stages of my earliest, formal religious training: What we called "witnessing" to friends, organizing evangelistic tent meetings, going to Bible college, doing missionary work in Southeast Asia. It describes the effect that spiritual experience had on my very rational worldview. Finally, these middle chapters explore the idea that it is often necessary to move beyond or outside of the faith of our parents in order to find our own spiritual self.

In Part Three, I describe my aborted pursuit of a monastic vocation, studying for the priesthood, my search for happiness and love, and arguments with my past. Each chapter title is a phrase from a poem I admire, expressing a spiritual idea that has defined my journey. For example, the eighth-century Chinese poet Han Shan wrote: "I've made elixirs and tried to become immortal / I've read the classics and written odes / and now I've retired to Cold Mountain / to lie in a stream and wash out my ears." Emily Dickinson provides the other four, helping me to express what is difficult to say.

In this book I write a great deal about my mother and father. It is important to me to say a brief something about that. They did not think that they were raising a fundamentalist, and in many ways, they didn't.

I once heard a theory about the transmission of beliefs from one generation to the next that posited a frequent skip. In other words, kids often look to their grandparents for the subtleties of what to think, who to be, and what is valuable. This is one explanation that sociologists use for why generations seem to constantly react to each other. I know that many of the things I did as a young adult shocked my mother and father as much as they did others who were close to me at the time. In many ways, I was schooled in fundamentalism as one would seek an ideal from the past.

It always sounds foolish to me when I hear someone remark that they used to be religious, used to be observant, used to be Lutheran, and so on. I even have a friend who likes to say "I used to be Jewish," which sounds really funny because for most people being Jewish is not something you can opt out of. It is like my grandmother who pretended she was no longer Italian when the childhood pain of being different was too great. Her immigrant family even changed the spelling of their last name, as many do. But, for the person intently raised in specific faith, there is no real way to get out of it. You cannot abandon it cleanly or completely. You may try to leave it behind, but it really cannot be done. Thank God. I would not be able to find my way with God today if I didn't try to understand where I've come from and what I learned there.

Throughout the book, I try to explain my struggles with dichotomies, times when I have felt pulled in (at least) two directions. These dichotomies exist in every healthy, evolving, spiritual person. We will always have elements of different sides or tendencies struggling inside and pulling at us. The pull of these seemingly opposed forces (perhaps they really are not in such opposition) is exactly the kind of tension that makes our experiences real and growing.

Jon M. Sweeney
West Hartford, Vermont

part one

just as I am

the most important decision
in fundamentalism

Just as I am, without one plea
but that thy blood was shed for me,
and that thou bid'st me come to thee,
O Lamb of God, I come, I come!
—"Just as I Am," a hymn by Charlotte Elliott

When I was five, I knelt with my father in the living room of our house to ask Jesus into my heart. Phrase by phrase, I repeated after my dad: "Dear heavenly Father . . . I realize that I am a sinner . . . and I ask for your forgiveness. . . . I want to change and become a new person. . . . I ask you to come into my heart." My mother sat nearby, beaming with pride. I was happy too, because I knew what had happened. God the

Father was writing my name in the Book of Life at the moment the words passed my lips.

I knelt like I had seen it done by others—as my dad showed me how. I clasped my hands together tightly before my face, lips resting on my knuckles. Squeezing my eyes closed, I tried to concentrate on my sin and why Jesus had to die for me. I was no different from those who actually nailed the long nails into Jesus' slender hands, I told myself; I killed him too, with my disobedience. If it were only to save me from my unrighteousness, Jesus would have given himself up to die. I was that important and also that guilty.

I can guess what you might be thinking: But it wasn't too much for a five-year-old to take in. There is no time like early childhood to really internalize sin and wickedness.

From where I knelt, on both knees on a throw rug in our tiny suburban Chicago home, I was in the center of the universe. We lived in Wheaton, Illinois, where there probably were more churches per capita than in any other city in America. Twenty-five miles to the east were the shores of Lake Michigan, and not far from Gino's Pizza and the Drake Hotel sat Moody Bible Institute on North LaSalle Avenue where my dad worked. In the outermost ring were the planets that rotated around me out of love—grandparents, aunts and uncles, neighbors, missionary and pastor friends.

On the afternoon of my conversion, my mother wrote the date in my new Bible. "Jonathan Mark became a Christian on September 3, 1972." No day in my young life mattered as much as this one. Every member of our family was now sanctified, set aside, holy in the eyes of God. If Christ would return today to gather up all true Christians, I would join my entire family to meet in the air. Yesterday, I would have been left behind.

My brother, who is two years older, prayed the same prayer with my father two years earlier as I looked on. My earliest memories are of pestering each of my parents, pleading for the right to do the same thing. "Why can't I?" I would whine. My father explained that it was important for me to first understand the enormity of what I was doing.

So I had decided to watch carefully in church, at home, and in the homes of my parents' friends. I learned to see how people behaved when they were talking with God, and talking about God. I learned what type of voice they used, their cadence and tone, and what subjects they emphasized and avoided. It was clear to me that sounding like you meant what you were saying was very important. Whatever you said with conviction, stood a better chance of being understood as sincere.

Young children being involved in religion is nothing new. The current Dalai Lama (Tenzin Gyatso) was born in 1935 in remote Tibet. Just two years later, Buddhist lamas, or spiritual leaders, were providentially led to his family home to determine if the infant could identify personal items of the last Dalai Lama, who had just died. When the boy answered their questions satisfactorily, he was soon declared the next Dalai Lama. Only three years later, Gyatso was "ruling" Tibet from the royal palace in Lhasa at the age of five. A generation ago, it was common in some churches in the American South for children to be called on to preach at very young ages. Somehow older folks figured that they had something to say, or that they had the spirit to say what God told them to say with feeling. Jesus taught the scholars in the synagogue while only a boy—his mother and father found him there—and, according to Catholic tradition, Mary couldn't have been too annoyed with his precociousness because she had done the same thing as a little girl.

When I was a child, my favorite Bible character was the boy Samuel. He was only five or so years old when his mother "lent him to the LORD." Hannah had conceived Samuel as a result of tearful petitions to God, before the priest of the temple, Eli. (Her husband had another wife who had already borne him children.) Hannah made a promise to God that, if her request for a male child was remembered, "I will give him to the LORD all the days of his life."

Samuel joined Eli, and they lived alone in the temple. Samuel spent the rest of his days doing the work of the Lord. Hannah, meanwhile, was rewarded with five more children to replace the special one that she had given to God.

It soon became clear that Samuel was to be a prophet. Visions were not widespread in those days, the Scriptures say, but Samuel began to have them. He was asleep at night when he heard someone urgently calling his name. There was power in those words. Samuel ran to Eli to respond, calling out, "Here am I." But Eli told him to go back to sleep; no one was calling him. This happened again and again until Eli knew that something special was happening to the boy. "Therefore Eli said unto Samuel, 'Go, lie down; and it shall be, if he call thee, that thou shalt say, 'Speak, LORD; for thy servant heareth.'" Samuel did as he was told, and from that day forward, God spoke directly to him.

God didn't talk much to me when I was five or six, but I knew that he was listening. Fundamentalism taught me that God was so close as to be inside my body, my heart. With my active childhood imagination, this theology germinated into lively spiritual experiences. I often saw God the Father and Jesus or John the Baptist above me, just hanging around, listening. Most often, they were in the sky, like cumulus clouds hovering above me feigning to communicate. One of the hymns that we sang in church pleaded, "Let the fire and cloudy pillar lead me. . . ." I remember having a vivid sense one day at dusk out on the open water of Lake Huron, of seeing God and his friends looking very serious in the skies above our boat, high in the sky. That strange experience helped me to understand William Blake's engravings when I encountered them later, in school. God was that dreadfully old man with a long beard; what was most real in the world was not of the world. God's presence didn't always comfort me; that time it scared me.

The Holy Spirit was my secret friend. The Bible teaches that the Holy Spirit is the Comforter, and for me as a child, the Holy Spirit felt comforting and friendly when Jesus and God the Father felt severe. I played alone a lot as a young child, most often in my room. I spent many Sunday afternoons with the Holy Spirit in my bedroom with the door closed. We talked quietly, but mostly he listened as I narrated the day's events or involved him in my games.

I was fascinated with the crucifixion of Jesus, which my Sunday school teacher discussed each week in some way. The passion of Christ—the stages from his arrest to his humiliation to his trial and then death— enthralled my imagination. Jesus knew every kid's nightmare: to be taken away, stripped naked, beaten up, pointed at, and laughed at. And somehow I knew that I had done it to him.

So, I experimented, playing in order to understand something complex. On those Sunday afternoons, I would close my door and strip my action figures naked, leaving Batman, Aquaman, and G. I. Joe to hang on crosses of my own design, easy to create with Lincoln Logs. I didn't simulate the agony of a crucifixion, the nailing of the spikes through their hands and feet, for example, only because I was too young to have seen any graphic Jesus movies. The early church actually didn't view the crucifixion as a dark and painful event, either. The earliest images of Jesus on the cross do not show him hanging, but superimposed, emphasizing the willing gift of love he gave, there. So, too, my crucified men were fairly unimpressive, dispassionately attached, staring out at me.

Looking at these embarrassments on the floor of my room, I would do what I now know to have been some kind of meditation. I would sit quietly gazing at them, thinking on Jesus and his sacrifice, praying with as deep a sorrow as I could muster. I learned this meditation practice in church, during the long periods of time that our pastor would take to, as we said, "prompt the Spirit to move," before offering the invitation to people to become Christians. This was standard fare in fundamentalist churches. The organ would play softly while the pastor spoke melodiously into the microphone, urging all in the congregation to consider their sinfulness, sometimes explaining the details of how Christ died. All together, I must have spent hundreds of hours with the intensity of a Jesuit concentrating empathy toward the pain, sacrifice, and sorrow of Christ. The intensity allowed me to feel the pain of nails in my hands and wish that I was in Jesus' place.

My school friends were very different from me. They didn't take these things as seriously as I did, and I didn't exactly let on what I was thinking, either. Church and school were worlds apart. At school, I learned and messed around in equal measure just like my friends. The only occasions when religion entered our conversations were when I would ask my Catholic buddies why they do those curious things, like crossing themselves and eating fish on Fridays. But at church on

Sunday mornings, Sunday evenings, and Wednesday nights, I often felt like I belonged to something set apart, something special.

We were not religious at our church. Our pastor made a clean distinction between being religious and being Christian. We were not practicing a religion, he said. People who practiced religions were not people with faith. Religion, he said, was the ultimate idol, and faith in Jesus made it unnecessary. For this reason, we were Baptist but not denominational Baptists. If the Southern Baptists are on the ideological right and American Baptists are on the ideological left—independent Baptists are nowhere in between. Independent Baptist churches are guided by their senior pastors, always men, and nearly always men of single-minded, fundamentalist vision.

My two grandfathers were both independent Baptist preachers for fifty years. They taught me that you don't need religion, denominations, or priests. If you look clearly and honestly at yourself in the presence of God, they used to tell me, you have all the spiritual direction you need. On any issue, if tradition was offered as support of truth, we knew that truth was elsewhere. Even more certainly, we knew that those whose belief was based on tradition had been duped, and they needed our help.

Our focus was not on church tradition, but on doctrine. And learning our doctrines was more of an emotive task than an intellectual one. To feel them inside of you was the real test of understanding. For this reason, I preferred Sunday evening church over Sunday morning, since Sunday mornings were difficult times to pay attention. I wiggled a lot and made paper airplanes with the attendance cards in the pew holders. When the children's time came, we all shuffled quietly out of the sanctuary and downstairs for Bible stories. Definitely not a time of reflecting inwardly on doctrinal truths.

But on Sunday evenings, the mystery of knowing God personally and intimately was clearly felt in the room. We saw God's face on the face of the people that we met. The service would begin with hymn singing—we sang loud, moving songs led by a song-leader behind the pulpit. He would motion for the organ or the piano to begin and then continue using his hand like a conductor uses a baton with an orchestra. Sometimes he would pause between verses and we would all go completely silent. Slowly intoning the next few words that we were about to sing, in his deep voice he then would plead, "With feeling, now!" We responded by singing louder and with more emotion, and I loved it. We didn't rock like the great African-American churches in downtown Chicago, but I remember loving my dad most when he was singing next to me in church. He was loud and melodious and he meant it, and I tried to sing out strong and mean it, too.

"Their singing caused him to believe in the presence of the Lord; indeed, it was no longer a question of belief, because they made that presence real," wrote James Baldwin in *Go Tell It on the Mountain*.

"Something happened to their faces and their voices, the rhythm of their bodies, and to the air they breathed; it was as though wherever they might be became the upper room, and the Holy Ghost was riding on the air."

After fifteen to twenty minutes of singing, our hearts were wide open. Then, the pastor asked for testimonies from the congregation: personal tellings of sin, journey, and return. Three or four people of the congregation would take turns standing where they were to say where they had come from and declare where they were headed with the help of Christ. Men would talk about how they had avoided God for so long but now they were here in the pews by God's grace; twenty-somethings would stand and re-dedicate their lives to following Christ after years of unfaithfulness using drugs, partying, disobeying parents; mothers would speak of their wayward sons. I would often cry because the speakers would cry, triggered like seeing someone yawn.

Fundamentalism taught me first of all that there is one decision more important than any other in life: to follow Christ. Through the experience of fundamentalist worship, I learned something equally as important: God's forgiveness means that we may always change, turn completely around, start over, become reborn. Strong emotion was more evidence of God at work inside of us. The Gospel story of the return of the prodigal son, in fact, made perfect sense to me because I knew him. I was him.

The feeling in the sanctuary was electric even though the building itself was as drab as could be, as nondescript as a recreation hall, or a senior center. Before services began, when people had yet to fill the room, I used to lean back in my pew and count the monotonous, gray, wooden slats of the roof. But, the congregation at worship would light it up like a campfire. Without any wild gifts of the Spirit—such as those practiced in the Assemblies of God church down the road—the sparks of faith still seemed to rise. Sparks in our mouths as we sang. Sparks from the Bibles opened on our laps. Sparks on the toes of my shoes as I walked up front, before the bare altar, to recommit my life (again and again) to Christ.

Some of the best times in church were when one of my grandfathers, or my dad, was leading the service. I remember once sitting in the pew in Romeoville, Illinois, as my Grandpa Turner preached. His fat, worn, black Scofield Bible shook in his left hand like a fish that had just hit the surface of the clear water on its way to the boat. He stalked the stage punching out his three points of expository doctrine. Always three points: "Easy to remember, easy to apply." The congregation sat still, like me, waiting for what might happen.

"Jesus Christ came to suffer and die!" he yelled. "He came not to be served, but to serve, and to give his life as a ransom for many! Are you one of that many? Amen? Do I hear 'Amen'?" He always asked that last Amen as a question.

I said "Amen" myself, along with many of the men in the congregation. It was a sign of my seriousness. And I went forward when the altar call was given. The altar call was the time in the service when the people were asked to make a decision for God—one of those life-altering moments—and to evidence that decision by walking to the front of the church and telling someone else about it. Deacons and other volunteers waited at the front. That night, I answered the call, not to be saved—I had done that when I was five—but to re-commit my life to following Jesus. I left my seat during the first verse of *Just As I Am*, the hymn that we so often sang during altar calls, and I was standing up front, looking up at my grandpa, when the third verse ended. I can still remember the rush of adrenaline in my limbs, the warm feeling in my cheeks.

Most fundamentalists don't answer these "altar calls" over and over, as I found myself doing. Technically, once is enough. Bam! You're forgiven, saved! But fundamentalism taught me the beauty and certainty of knowing God is there to receive us, and embrace us, always. I needed more.

In high school, years later, I remember reading a Flannery O'Connor story in which at the end, the main character, a contemptuous old woman, is shot dead by a drifter. Her mind opens to grace only once and only at that moment. For the first, and unfortunately, the last time, she suddenly sees things clearly. As she dies, her killer says, "She would have been a good woman if it had been somebody there to shoot her every minute of her life." I must have walked forward during two dozen altar calls as a child, full of emotion and fervor, needing reminders of grace. On each occasion, my decision felt final, paramount, life-giving, life-changing. Today, I sometimes think that I needed all of those altar calls and decisions. I still do.

two

angels in the trees

my unusual religious imagination

The written letters kill, but the Spirit gives life.
—2 Corinthians 3.6

I was not taught to be a mystic—in fact, quite the opposite. For fundamentalists, faith was something clear and unaddled, like listening carefully in order to follow directions properly, or simply getting your facts straight. We found the answers to our questions about life in the pages of the Bible, Old and New Testaments. We believed that everyone who read the Bible without prejudice would see things exactly as we did. The Holy Spirit would make sure of it.

But, in reality, our lives were full of mysticism. We believed that God was active inside of us—listening, speaking, guiding—creating what we called a sanctified, individual conscience and will. This mystical new identity was the only safe guide to correct understanding and reliable decision-making.

Fundamentalism shares this idea of an interior guide, or light, with other Christian denominations. In fact, the intense feeling and expression of the indwelling of Christ is a mysticism that is distinctively important for many Christians. It is spirituality that is embodied. We know it in our hearts; we feel it as surely as our deepest feelings; and we also put it into practice. Christ in the heart is sure guidance. This did not seem arbitrary to me in practice when I was a child, but I know how willy-nilly it can appear and sound to others.

Recently, in my book publishing work, I had occasion to spend a June weekend for three consecutive years exhibiting our books at the International New Age Trade Show in Denver, Colorado. The purpose of the show is for retailers to peruse the displays of publishers and other vendors and to order goods to sell in their shops. I saw things on that exhibit floor that I never saw at other trade shows: Aromatherapy, Tarot card readings, full-body messages. But I will always remember one conversation in particular. On this occasion, a retailer stood in front of our stand of books and, as I described each one in some detail, he would look down at something hanging from his neck, examining it closely until I stopped talking. He would then look up at me and say, "I'll take two," or, "I'll take one," or, "I'll pass on that one." I realized, after a short while, that he was examining a necklace crystal before making his decisions. At about this point in the conversation, one of the buyer's friends came up to him from the side aisle, pointed at the crystal, and said, "I love watching you do that!" And the man replied, "It is the only way that I can know anything for certain."

Similarly, my certainty as a child was based on what I was told by others but also on what I grew to feel inside. I knew that God was very close. I talked to Jesus quietly in my soul, and he whispered back, and occasionally, as in the stories of the medieval mystics, there was rhapsody, and even tears.

These emotions of faith were never taught to me. For the most part, I lived in a simple place that was uncluttered and uncomplicated. Everything had a purpose—"teleology," as the philosophers say—and it all made sense without feelings and emotions. Eating was for the purpose of strengthening the soul, the temple of the body. Recreation was time for building relationships. Study—to show yourself worthy. Work—duty.

The changes in attitudes and perspectives that came with the 1960s seemed to have had little effect on life in my hometown of Wheaton, Illinois, or on my parents. Our house sat in the middle of a small suburban plot of grass in the middle of a quiet street of asphalt driveways, lampposts, and small culverts. I played outside with my friends, and my parents had little reason to worry about my safety. On summer nights, my brother and I would be gone for several hours at a time, taking in the entire neighborhood of backyards and open fields in our games. We rode our bicycles down the middle of city streets before anyone had thought of wearing a bicycle helmet. We lived in the suburbs before anyone expected much danger or contrast there.

In church we had certain expectations—we made unspoken and informal vows against smoking, drinking, swearing, dancing. These were the Bill of Rights that most conservative churches added onto the Ten Commandments. Most of my friends' families agreed that these things were wrong and they were to have nothing to do with life in our neighborhood. Anyone who was caught doing them became known as a troublemaker.

As a young child, I felt that my life was under constant divine surveillance. The "eyes of God" has always been a tangible metaphor to my mind and imagination, a mix of excited and frightening. God watched with unblinking constancy as I played, walked to school, obeyed and disobeyed my parents. Those frightening words that kids sing about Santa Claus, "He sees you when you're sleeping. He knows when you're awake. . . ." only cemented the all-knowing grandfatherly image of God for me. My God was Yahweh who is praised by King David: "He telleth the number of the stars; he calleth them all by their names. Great is our Lord, and of great power: his understanding is infinite."

I remember being quite sure in the first grade that God even used the television set to keep an eye on me inside the house. I would quietly interrogate the tube when I was alone in the room: "What do you *want*?" and I would sometimes hide behind the furniture when the glare felt particularly intense. My world was a towering cylinder of divine attention, a tornado circling down. A Siberian shaman may move freely through to the upper and down to the lower worlds at his pleasure, but I was the simple object of God's Eyes.

Our unique brand of mysticism rejected most of the miracles that characterize popular Catholic piety. Our church did not teach about the great Christian saints. There were no legends of St. George and the dragon, St. Francis and the wolf, or St. Lucia and her eyes. We rejected any miracles that were supposed to have happened after the era of the New Testament; the time for that sort of thing had passed with the last apostles, we believed. If I had mysteriously received one of the stigmata one evening my mother would have scrubbed my palms for hours wondering what kind of mess I'd gotten myself into. There was no point in confusing faith with that sort of mystical fantasy.

But rejecting the Catholic imagination did not eliminate our need for mysticism. We all have a need for something beyond, something transcendent. We developed our own versions, and in many respects, our fundamentalism was as full of mysticism as any branch of faith.

My own imagination thrived in an environment where God was always watching. For me, there were angels in the trees. The birds sang me songs on my walks to and from school. The willow trees hung low to catch up little kids in their spindly branches, just as the insect-eating plant in my room caught ants and flies. Clouds followed me and God was in them. I saw the faces of Moses, the one who saw God; the woman from Bethany who wept on the feet of Jesus; the apostles James and John and Peter when I passed strangers in the street. The stories of the Bible were alive for me.

Bible story books from home blended in my imagination with subjects discussed in elementary school. Abraham Lincoln's long walk to return a mislaid penny exemplified trust just as the tale told in 2 Kings 5, of Naaman, the proud Syrian soldier, who obeyed Elisha, the prophet of Israel, by dipping himself seven times in the river Jordan to cure his leprosy. In second grade, we studied Johnny Appleseed. I imagined his legs like Jesus' legs: what else could explain how Johnny walked so far? I planted trees in our backyard and wished that I could wander far from home. I also dreamed that my feet would become like Jesus' so I could walk on the water, and I prayed for faith. It was Peter's lack of confidence that had caused him to sink below the surface; I vowed that that would never happen to me.

My religious imagination also led me to dream of my vocation. What great adventures would I undertake for God? When I was nine, a missionary named Don Richardson came to speak at our church about his work in the jungles of Irian Jaya, a remote part of Indonesia. He was promoting his new book *Peace Child*, that chronicled what it was like to leave the comfort and security of American life and travel to the Third World for Christ.

Richardson showed slides of the people of the Dani tribe, the largest ethnic group in Irian Jaya, and explained how he lived among them in a tropical forest. None of the tribe's members had yet asked Jesus into their heart, he said, but it took many years to first gain their trust. He explained some of their rituals, such as cannibalism and worship of a pig, the clan's most prized possession. He explained that other missionaries to the region had been killed, their heads cut off and stuck on the ends of poles for good luck, or their skulls used as pillows. I was enthralled. I remember begging my dad to let me buy his book after the talk. When Don Richardson signed my new copy I proudly said, "I am going to be a missionary, too!"

I devoured *Peace Child*, memorizing the black and white photographs of the cannibals with their captions, dreaming of what it would be like to run through the jungle with them, hunting wild boar. It all scared me, but as the thrill of a roller coaster is scary. I wanted the book and its message to become a part of me, as the prophet Jeremiah might have felt when he said to God: "Thy words were found, and I did eat them."

I became convinced that missionary work would be my life's vocation. At school I could think of little else for weeks, daydreaming of my adventures to come and the seriousness that would bring meaning to my life for God. Recess in fourth grade was usually spent outdoors, and I was a pretty good kickball player, but on the Monday after that Sunday talk, I begged special permission to spend recess in the school library.

"What are you planning to do?" asked Mr. Hendrikson my teacher with a suspicious look on his face. He often looked that way as he constantly shifted his weight painfully from side to side, the result of childhood polio in his legs and hips.

"Research," I said with confidence, and then added, "There are some things I need to look up in the *Encyclopaedia Britannica*." The EB lent credibility to my case.

For three days I worked in the school library learning more about missionaries. I read about the apostle Paul and his missions to the Gentiles, Saint Patrick's work in Ireland, David Livingston's adventures in Africa, and Hudson Taylor in China in the late nineteenth century.

When school friends asked me what I was doing, I shrugged it off, embarrassed to tell them the truth. My friends did not attend my church and I never did figure out how to tell them that they needed a missionary as much as the people of Irian Jaya. How do you break that news to your nine-year-old friends? As our pastor said each autumn in a series of sermons on Paul's Epistle to the Romans, in order to go to heaven you must "confess with thy mouth" that you are a sinner and invite Jesus into your heart. If you completely give yourself to God day after day, God will show you clearly those things that he has for you. My friends hadn't done any of that. I know because I asked them and they didn't know what I was talking about.

I had a lot of guilt about what a lousy witness for God I was at school. I knew that I didn't try hard enough to save people. In my father's day, born-again Christian kids showed their difference and devotion by proudly carrying their Bibles to and from school each day. We called it "setting ourselves apart from the world." Carrying a Bible was a simple way for a child to do it. My dad suggested this to me, but the prospect of comments from other kids was simply too embarrassing for me to face. Somehow, I vaguely hoped that people would see the glow of light coming from the God inside my body—so that I wouldn't have to explain it.

But my Sunday school teachers soon taught me to tell people, to "witness" to both friends and strangers, telling them that God had died for them. Training for this work was my responsibility as a Christian, they said, but as someone who had been identified as a future leader, it was even more important for me to practice.

We also learned the importance of witnessing at Bible camp each summer. Around the campfire at night, somewhere in the woods near Lake Michigan, we listened to our camp counselors tell stirring tales of the first disciples sent to all corners of the globe after the resurrection and ascension of Christ. We learned to be "faithful disciples" ourselves, following Jesus. One of the counselors played the guitar while we sang a common chorus:

Seek ye first the kingdom of God
and His righteousness,
and all these things shall be added unto you.
Hallelu-hallelu-jah.

The flickering of the fire offered just enough light for us to write notes in the margins of our study Bibles, and to occasionally clap them closed on any mosquitoes that happened to land on their open pages.

My great-grandmother was a great model of witnessing. She was known throughout her mobile home park, her church, and her town as a Christian who was joyful in telling others about Jesus. I remember one occasion when I stayed overnight at her home. She had insisted to my parents that I not just visit, but sleep there, which was a scary proposition. One thing I am certain of is that she had no toothpaste in the house because she had no teeth; her dentures sat in a glass jar on the kitchen counter at nighttime. Using her baking soda for tooth-brushing that night made more of an impression on me than did her exhortations to "Tell people about Jesus!" and "Spread his love!"

But it was not love for others that eventually motivated me to work harder at "saving souls"; it was the threat of God's wrath. I knew from Sunday school that Jesus had told a parable about sheep and goats that mirrored what would happen at the end of time. The sheep were those who did what they were supposed to do and the goats were those who did not. The sheep would go to be with Jesus, their shepherd, while the goats would be sent away from his face forever. The Gospel of Matthew put it like this: "Then shall he say also unto them on the left hand, Depart from me, ye cursed, into everlasting fire, prepared for the devil and his angels."

"You can obey God out of love or fear," my pastor used to say. "God prefers the former, but the latter will do, too." The most awful chasms of fire painted by Hieronymus Bosch are the visions of what I was told separated those who believed from those who did not. Hell was a real place for me, and its horrors were palpable. If in medieval theology hell had various levels and perpetual punishments, for me it was also a stench hanging around most of the people I knew.

James Baldwin wrote about people who are "goats" in *Go Tell It on the Mountain*: "[T]heir thoughts were not of God, and their way was not God's way. They were in the world, and of the world, and their feet laid hold on Hell."

Guilt and fear were not enough to convince me to do something missionary-like about the fate of the people around me, so I decided that I could go far away and do my duty with less embarrassment. I was soon convinced—I cannot remember exactly why—that India needed me the most. As I read further about missionary work, I learned that the largest cities in India, like Calcutta and Bombay, already had missionaries. I even discovered that photographs of some of them were pinned to a bulletin board in our church foyer. "Pray for Us" it read in a banner of construction paper across the top. Our church supported their work financially. So after ruling out these more urban places as the hub of my future missionary activity, I used the only technique that I knew to decide on another: I closed my eyes and dropped my index finger on the glossy encyclopedia map. . . . Benares.

I learned all of those things that I imagined one had to know to be a missionary in the city of Benares, India, writing it all down in my journal and memorizing it. Average annual rainfall, average temperature in June and December, primary agriculture, population, major religion. Benares, a/k/a. Varanasi, "the holy city," was the home of Hindu University, a pilgrimage place on the Ganges River and a preferred place for the devout to die. The people there believed that dying on the ghats, or platforms, by the river in Benares ensured nirvana and an end to the cycles of rebirth. Benares was also the place where the Buddha had preached for the first time after achieving enlightenment. My work was cut out for me, I thought. When I described my ambitious missionary plans, I was very much admired by the adults in my clan.

I declared my plans publicly by my baptism when I was nine. "Yes, I have accepted Jesus Christ as my Savior. I did that when I was five," I said into the portable microphone during my public interview with the pastor from the baptismal tank. My legs were quickly numb from the cold water. The white gown I had to wear kept floating up around my waist, exposing my underwear to the choir members sitting within view.

"Do you plan to live your life according to God's ways, in obedience to his will?" my pastor asked, his own gown sticking somehow neatly to his thighs. He was in the tank with me.

"Yes I do. In fact, I plan to become a missionary," I replied, my voice cracking with nervousness, cold, and excitement. The congregation applauded quietly, and I even heard a few "Amens."

"I now baptize you in the name of the Father, the Son, and the Holy Spirit," he intoned, and he dunked me backwards into the icy water. That was the moment that adults began expecting great things from me.

Fundamentalism also taught me to expect great things of myself. I treasure the ways that fundamentalism taught me to take my faith seriously. I learned to imagine God at work in the world, and to imagine my own essential role in the divine plan. What I intended, studied, said, and did, mattered; a spiritual life was made of these many small, deliberate things.

■ ■ ■ ■ ■ ■ ■ three

medicine men

my gurus

We receive more than we can ever give; we receive it from the past, on which we draw with every breath, but also . . . from the source of the mystery itself, which religious people call Grace.
—Edwin Muir

I squeezed my eyes tightly shut and soon saw only a flood of tiny points of light. The harder I squeezed, the more sorrow I was able to feel. Soon, my jaw hurt from clenching my teeth. Focus your mind on a vivid scene, my pastor said: the torture and death of Jesus. He died in your place. Your sins he carried to Golgotha. Your sins were nailed into his hands. And you are just like one of those in the crowd who chanted, "Crucify him!"

I imagine myself plucked from a crowd of kids and thrown to the ground, held there by large, dirty hands, as others prepare the wooden cross for my own crucifixion. I was born guilty of sin deserving of death. But then, at that almost cinematic moment, I hear God's voice from heaven telling Jesus to stand in my place, and he does. Dirty hands release their grips and I stand up, walking away bewildered and sad. I repeat to myself: They should have taken me.

Such were my meditations on the cross, infantile but vivid. But it wasn't enough; it never was. I could not empathize like I knew I should. I could not feel the pain as it must have really felt. Even when I dug my fingernails into my palms I could not feel all that I knew I needed to feel. I couldn't match the gravity of Christ's sacrifice.

Anthropologists study the "local codes" that govern the experience of faith in gesture, movement, and speech in distinctive religious environments. They spend months or years among native people in exotic locales in order to determine as best they can what it means in that culture when someone kneels, or presses palms together looking heavenward, or digs in the dirt in search of nothing in particular.

As a ten-year-old, I wanted very much to be a spiritual leader in my tradition, one who had experienced God's presence. Already at that age I understood the "local codes," the power of leading as it was demonstrated in public. Strong voice, certain demeanor, studied answers to any questions of doubt, hands that point to heaven and to others. My father was powerful, and his father before him, not like priests who were feared in the Middle Ages, holding the Eucharist or the cross like a weapon against the unfaithful, but because they knew how to speak with the voice of God. They knew certainty, and it both poured forth and boiled within, as though from the Spirit that gives authority and prophecy.

I wanted to fulfill my family legacy. I was taught to be certain, initiated into the Christian tradition as one who would someday lead (preach and teach) so that others would follow. God intended me to lead, I was told; that much was clear, and the world out there needs more leaders. Until I was about twenty years old there was nothing else in my life that I so clearly understood: there was a spiritual need and I would meet that need.

In those pre-pubescent years, for a short time I became a model for a popular Christian photographer based in our town. He would pay my mother five dollars for an hour of sitting, and the prints would later appear in advertisements for Christian products. Years later, I still saw my image in ads for Bible covers and spiritual magazines aimed at evangelical women. The same photographer was also hired to shoot a short film about kids struggling for acceptance among their peers. I was chosen for the lead part, but failed in the first scene when I was unable to look unhappy, demonstrably frowning, in the middle of a crowd of my cheerful playmates at Sunday school. I kept giggling, take after take, and was replaced an hour or so later by one of my more dour friends.

Fundamentalism showed me the value of older friends and mentors. I had ready models of kindness, generosity, leadership, and hospitality—both in my own family and in the extended family that church became for me. There was no limit, we believed, to what God could do in and through a person's life.

In my reading about missionaries, I encountered photographs of Hindu holy men in India. These images of naked or near-naked men with wild hair and eyes never really shocked me. We had our own holy people, our spiritual healers and communicators of different sorts. Our religious culture was based on images, just as Catholic and Orthodox churches are built around images of a different sort. In fact, a steady stream of images and icons came in and out of my life through our church, my family, and my father's work at the Moody Bible Institute in Chicago. Some of them created lasting memories for me.

For instance, I'll never forget the gospel singer who had survived a fire that burned 90 percent of the skin on his body. "His head had expanded to the size of a basketball," his brochure read, "when he first arrived at the hospital." Gruesome photos showed his story of faith and trust in God, making his inspirational hymn singing all the more moving, and his albums sold briskly.

Then there was Joni Eareckson, a paraplegic at age eighteen as a result of a diving accident. Everyone, it seemed, read her memoir, *Joni*, and she became famous, a star in the evangelical Christian world. Her paintings, executed with a brush held in her teeth (the 1970s cover of *Joni* pictured her smiling, long bangs, brush in teeth), were beautiful and a signal of a fighting, faithful spirit within that damaged body. We heard her speak when she came through Wheaton, as all of the stars of the fundamentalist world did.

Dr. George Speake may have made the most lasting impression on me. As one who traveled the world demonstrating how even the advancements of science have God's fingerprints all over them, Speake was known as the man who would send one million volts of electricity through his body, an act he performed for decades in front of live audiences on behalf of the Moody Bible Institute of Science. A small, round, elevated platform was placed on a stage and he stood on it. Connected to the platform were wires that transmitted high voltage electric currents through his body. The lights of the auditorium would be dimmed, and the switch turned on. People would gasp and even scream as you could see the jagged lines of electricity surging out of Speake's fingertips as rays of red and yellow light. An assistant would toss him two-by-four pieces of wood, one for each hand, and the wood would burn while held in his hands. Like a circus sideshow, the purpose of this performance, which I saw many times in Chicago and again at the summer Olympic Games in Montreal, was to draw a crowd—in order to then, as we said, share the Good News of Jesus with the captive audience.

As I was trying to find my own niche in the world of Christian leaders, I was most impressed by the great preachers. I heard Stephen Olford, the eloquent Englishman; James Boice, the intellect from Philadelphia; and many evangelists and prophecy preachers such as J. Vernon McGee, George Sweeting, Luis Palau, George Verwer, and others. And, of course, there was Billy Graham, whose sermon I was once thrilled to be responsible for photocopying a few days before he delivered it at Moody Bible Institute's one hundredth anniversary celebration. It was printed in 26-point type—easier on Graham's eyes even then, before his Parkinson's disease set in—and styled in all CAPS, triple-spaced. I was a first-year student at Moody Bible Institute at the time, working also as a writer in the publicity department. Of course, I clan-destinely made a personal copy for possible future use.

My grandfathers were preachers, and came of age during the Depression, raised in what they'd describe as less-than-spiritual homes—one in Kansas, the other in Michigan. Grandpa Turner was fired with an evangelistic zeal by his local minister while in his teens. In 1928, he followed his young passion to the Moody Bible Institute, radio ministry, and book publisher in Chicago, where my own parents later attended and my dad later worked. Moody Bible Institute, or MBI, has been near the center of Christian fundamentalism for more than a century. Grandpa Turner wanted to be like the school's founder, Dwight L. Moody, a hardworking shoe salesman from New England who went on to preach before more people than any other figure in nineteenth-century America.

Grandpa Turner's education in fundamentalism was probably little different from my parents', and then little different from my own. For him, saving souls and separation from the world were the two marks of a good Christian. It is hard to imagine now that anybody in the 1940s was morally opposed to tuning into Benny Goodman and his orchestra on Saturday nights. But my grandpa was, and he didn't.

Grandpa Sweeney, on the other hand, started adulthood by marrying a beautiful Italian woman and establishing a successful insurance sales business. He was something of a swinger by the standards in Kansas in the 1930s, a dancer and a drinker, enjoying how far he had come from the poverty of his own father, who was a tenant farmer. An old photograph pictures Grandpa, then age four, standing beside his seated father. They are holding hands on the front porch of their tiny shack near Hammond, Kansas. The year is 1914, not a great year in the world. His father, my great-grandfather, is wearing dirty overalls, boots caked with mud, and a serious but sincere look on his very rugged face. "Do your chores," I can almost hear him telling my young grandfather. And, of course, like every kid everywhere since time began, Grandpa rebelled and for all of the years that I knew him forever tried to keep from getting dirt under his fingernails. No one ever saw my Grandpa Sweeney cut the lawn of his own suburban home in anything other than wingtips, slacks, and a button-down dress shirt.

But by the early 1940s, Grandpa Sweeney, too, was finally converted to Christianity and also on his way to Moody Bible Institute. With three young boys in tow, my father the youngest, the Sweeneys moved into married student housing on the North LaSalle Avenue campus in the summer of 1943.

For the rest of their lives after graduating from Bible college, my grandfathers were Baptist preachers of large churches in small towns like Troy, Michigan; New Philadelphia, Ohio; and Gresham, Oregon. My grandmothers always seemed satisfied to be defined as the wives of Baptist preachers.

My Grandpa Sweeney taught me to love good preaching. He used to rave about "tough old Harry Ironside" whom he heard preach regularly at Moody Memorial Church on LaSalle Avenue in Chicago during and after the Second World War. Ironside was never ordained and had almost no formal education, and this endeared him to people like my grandfathers. He preached from the heart and packed the large Moody Church to capacity for almost two decades.

Ironside was once called "the Archbishop of Fundamentalism," for the leadership he assumed over the movement. Reminiscing decades later, Dr. Ironside recounted the impact that hearing D. L. Moody himself preach, had had on him as a boy:

Mr. Moody . . . rose to his feet and began to plead with men to be reconciled to God. At first there was no movement, then he said abruptly, "Will every truly converted person in this building rise to your feet?" Possibly five thousand instantly arose. "Will all who were converted before you were fifteen years of age sit down?" Over half took their seats. "Now all who were saved before you were twenty please be seated." Probably half of those remaining obeyed him.

Then he went on in the same way, "All below thirty— forty—fifty." By that time a mere handful were still standing. "All below sixty." If my memory serves me aright, only three out of that vast throng continued to stand. "Now all saved before you were seventy," and the last were seated. It was a powerful object lesson, showing the importance of coming to Christ while young.

Moody pressed this home, then invited anxious souls to the inquiry-room. Many went in.

Another night I managed to get there early, with my mother and several of her friends. We sat only a few seats from the front, and so had a good view of Mr. Moody and the rest. I remember thinking, "He isn't very handsome." But when he preached on "Sowing and Reaping," his face lighted up, and he really seemed beautiful in his sincerity and kindly earnestness. . . . Again many went to the inquiry-room at Moody's invitation.

On the way home a gentleman in our party remarked, "He seems just a very ordinary man. I have heard many better preachers." "Yes," my mother answered, "but he wins souls!" I have often recalled this since. It was not remarkable eloquence or superior preaching ability that accounted for Moody's success. It was a life dominated by the Spirit of God, coupled with a certain native shrewdness that enabled him to understand the needs and hearts of men as few others have done.

During the war, Grandpa also admired Gabriel Heater, who began his daily radio broadcast at 6:30 p.m. with words the country longed to hear: "There is good news tonight!" Anecdotes such as these inspired me to model myself after the old guard. I remember impressing my Grandpa by reading and annotating three volumes of the sermons of Charles Spurgeon, the popular British preacher of the nineteenth century, when I was twelve. These were my gurus; this was my education.

In fundamentalism what was new was not nearly as valuable as what was old. One of our most popular hymns went, "Tell me the old, old story." But fundamentalism in America did not originate the idea that the truths of faith are a closed set. This idea is almost as old as the Church itself. The second-century theologian Tertullian for instance, once said: "We don't need curiosity after Christ, or investigation after the Gospel." Fundamentalism nurtures these ideas in our own time.

It is difficult today to imagine how I could *not* be a Christian after all the preaching I've heard. Thunderous, rhythmic word pounding the Spirit of God: its pulse is in me; like the gills in a fish, I've breathed with it. Just as we don't necessarily reason our way to love, we don't always choose our faith, either.

And perhaps we don't realize what a memory our senses have, and what a tug those memories can have on our behavior and on our deepest, spiritual selves.

I first saw the light and screamed as a baby in Christianity—and somewhere unspoken and unthought of, I remember and still believe. Today, though, what I no longer believe intellectually, my body and emotions still understand as faith. I get goose bumps when I hear old, familiar hymns. In fact, you could easily catch me tuning the AM dial late at night to find small-town preachers on my car radio. The sensuous, more than the dogma, binds me, like a slip knot, loosely but decisively to my religious place.

■ ■ ■ ■ ■ ■ ■ four

speaking the unspeakable
the power of language
in fundamentalism

I do not think you will have much difficulty in keeping the patient in the dark. . . . If any faint suspicion of your existence begins to arise in his mind, suggest to him a picture of something in red tights, and persuade him that since he cannot believe in that . . . he therefore cannot believe in you.

—Screwtape to his nephew, Wormwood,

in C. S. Lewis's *The Screwtape Letters*

Words have the power to help, hurt, and heal, according to how they are used. In the fundamentalism of my childhood, words also held intrinsic powers;

they stood like curtained doorways, ready to open out into programmed consequences.

Sin, too, was real in ways that were palpable. For all Christians, sin means "missing the mark," or falling short of the standard that God sets for us. But for us, in my church, sin was like barnacles on our sides. They would multiply if ignored, but just as easily, they could fall off completely. For me as a child, sin was like a removable organ; we had surgical procedures for making our bodies and souls healthy. Sin was a condition, not something that is stepped into temporarily, but something in our hearts, a piece of ourselves that we formerly loved and must cut out with a knife.

Sin was also real on the outside of us. It had a real, physical power apart from human beings, and we saw it as something to fight against. There were temples of sin (those of other faiths, particularly the ones that did not look anything like what faith and worship are supposed to look like), rooms considered to have an evil presence, and people who were permanently, spiritually lost. We tried desperately not to talk about the metaphysical stuff that was all around us, but denying its existence was unthinkable. Through C. S. Lewis's charming tales of an experienced devil advising his young devil-apprentice in *The Screwtape Letters* (quoted above), we understood perfectly that evil is real, even though most people are unaware of it, or are beguiled into believing otherwise.

Words had intrinsic power. The decision for Christ— to be born again—like the one I had made at age five in our living room, was not just speech, but tangible action taken against the onslaught of sin and evil. It was power-ful, initial-capped words versus powerful, initial-capped words: God over Satan. Fundamentalists use words as though they have the strength of action. Saying that you are born again means, actually, that you are.

In his many crusades, Billy Graham always concluded his sermons with an invitation just like this one:

> I am going to ask you to come. . . . You come—right now—quickly. I am going to ask you to get up out of your seats from all over the place—quietly and reverently—and come and stand here for a moment. Say, "Tonight I receive Christ. I give my life to Christ. I will serve and follow Him from this moment on." If you are with friends or relatives, they will wait for you. . . . It's an act of your will. You come right now! . . . You can make a decision tonight that will change your life. You can be born again and you'll never be the same.

In timeless, quick succession, words like this, words *declared*, words slashing like swords made our religious history happen: Words of rebellion against God's instructions in the Garden of Eden changed what it meant to know God, and then changed everyone and everything that came after it. Christ's words of acceptance of God's will on the cross, and his atoning sacrifice, broke the spell of sin that ruled after the Fall. Our words of inviting Christ to come inside of us altered our histories and our futures forever.

Assigning that sort of power to simple, everyday words led to many other word-powers. The name of Jesus took on great power for us. We were told that the first apostles exercised it to combat evil, and so did the priests in the film *The Exorcist* (1973). Healings in the name of Jesus—simply speaking the word *Jesus*—were used as combative against possessions of the devil. Though we did none of this in our church or in our family, we knew better than to discount the reality that it represented. We didn't see *The Exorcist* because of all of the obscenities, graphic violence, and sex, but we knew that the situations it explored were rooted in real possibilities. To even discuss the movie would be, to use an expression from Judaism, to tempt the evil eye. It frightened us deeply without even seeing it. Today, this all reminds me of the Harry Potter books and films in which the other wizards say to Harry with incredible *gravitas*, "We do not speak his name," whenever he attempts to ask a question about Voldemort, the leader of the wizards-gone-bad. Thirty years ago in my community, a series of novels or films about wizardry, no matter how seemingly entertaining or harmless, would have been banned as "demonic" in the strongest of terms. We wouldn't have wanted it thought about, let alone talked about.

Not only words, but numbers sometimes took on intrinsic significance, as well. "666" was the mark of the Beast, a number said to identify the Antichrist—the archenemy of the returning Christ—in the last days. Heavy metal bands would sometimes use the number as a sort of harmless insignia, or kitsch, but it was no laughing matter to me. I warned friends, in the stringent terms of an evangelist, against mingling with such popular music. But when I actually encountered the number, or an upside-down cross—on a T-shirt or a friend's album cover—I became immobilized, frightened to the seat of my pants.

One afternoon in junior high school, I heard a Christian apologist speak about the tangible evil in rock and roll music. He explained how bands such as The Rolling Stones and The Eagles were using subtle techniques to subliminally tweak teenage minds in favor of Satanism. He spun the Stones record, "Sympathy for the Devil" (1969) backwards and showed transcriptions on an overhead projector of what the lyrics purported to say when played that way. "This may seem relatively harmless when heard normally, but not when you uncover what they want you to unconsciously 'take in,'" he said. Kids were being enticed to play records backwards alone in their bedrooms, the apologist explained.

Then he showed close-ups from the photo spread inside of The Eagles' bestselling album *Hotel California* (1976), one of my favorites. One piece of the image appeared to be of a man standing at a window. The lecturer explained that the man pictured there was actually a renowned Satanist and a friend of the band. "You can see whom they are serving!" he exclaimed.

I was shaken and convinced that evil messages were infiltrating my normal defenses. As soon as I returned home that afternoon, I went to my brother's room and gathered up his Eagles cassette tapes. I took them outside to the asphalt driveway and smashed them into pieces with a hammer. The amazing guitar solos of Joe Walsh and Glenn Frey were not worth the terrifying prospect of making contact with the devil.

I explained it to Doug that night rather sheepishly. "He showed us how the music and the band and the secret message of the lyrics are satanic," I said, still feeling somewhat breathless. "I threw the pieces in the trash can," I concluded. I didn't even want Doug to see the plastic bits, again.

"Okay," he replied. How could he argue with that?

One of the scariest uses of words was the phrase we referred to as "the unforgivable sin." Great mystery surrounded this, and there was never clear consensus or even much discussion of what it could be, but Jesus introduced the concept in the Gospel of Matthew:

> Wherefore I say unto you, all manner of sin and blasphemy shall be forgiven unto men: but the blasphemy against the Holy Ghost shall not be forgiven unto men. And whosoever speaketh a word against the Son of man, it shall be forgiven him: but whosoever speaketh against the Holy Ghost, it shall not be forgiven him, neither in this world, neither in the world to come.

Luke captures the same incident, from a time when Jesus was speaking to the Pharisees, with these words: "And whosoever shall speak a word against the Son of man, it shall be forgiven him: but unto him that blasphemeth against the Holy Ghost it shall not be forgiven."

We didn't know what in the world that meant. It sure didn't seem that people were finding ways to speak ill of the Holy Ghost. Why bother? It must be something more subtle, we thought. Perhaps we were doing it and we didn't even intend to.

Medieval theologians wrote volumes on this topic. Thomas Aquinas, for instance, spent many pages of his masterwork, the *Summa Theologica*, on it. Augustine explained rather simply and matter-of-factly that the unforgivable sin is committed by he who obstinately refuses the forgiveness of sins—blasphemy against the Holy Ghost—even on his deathbed. This was a simple explanation, because we already knew that those who do not accept Christ as Savior "shall not be forgiven."

Many neuroses and much emotionally disturbed behavior has had its roots over the centuries in the unforgivable sin, when people have become convinced that they have committed this queen mother of all sins—whatever it might be. Our pastor urged us to understand that genuine salvation can never be taken away. The power of those words spoken, asking Jesus to come into our hearts, if genuinely offered to God, are effective for eternity. But, what if my words were not genuine, I asked myself? How would I know for sure?

My friends and I were convinced that the blasphemy of the unforgivable sin was what we also called "taking the Lord's name in vain," a type of swearing that is also blasphemy. Using words like *God* or *Jesus* or *Christ* was dangerous, when it was done flippantly. Words were powerful because their meanings were intrinsic. We were not Humpty Dumptys who said: "When I use a word it means just what I choose it to mean, neither more nor less." We didn't have the luxury of selecting what our words would mean; the meaning of every-thing preceded us.

One day, moments after falling headlong from my bicycle and skinning my knees on the gravel road, I screamed out, "Christ!" Heaven knows why I said it. I must have heard the Lord's name used this way on television. But the moment I said it I shuddered and the pain in my knees fell away. I was sure that I had committed the unforgivable sin.

In the end, Thomas Aquinas defined the one, true, unforgivable sin as despair. To be bereft of hope to the point of taking one's life is, for many others, the sin that God could never forgive. I had a friend in high school who committed suicide, and I prayed to God to let it go, to forget his sin, to regard him as out of his mind rather than the greatest of blasphemers.

Today, I wonder if the unforgivable sin is actually what happens when we have hardened ourselves to the point of spiritual numbness, when we offend the presence of the Holy Ghost inside of us. If we are going to love the Lord our God with all of our heart, mind, and spirit, that must mean that our lives and our words have to be full of meaning. The meaning doesn't have to precede us in the words themselves, but the meaning has to be in our lives and we have to be able to talk about it. Fundamentalism may have handicapped me in encountering the world, but it did transmit rich language and a lack of inhibition to use those words to express God's power in everyday life.

One of the most poignant scenes in literature must surely be from Shakespeare when MacBeth is recounting to his evil wife, the Lady MacBeth, how he has just murdered King Duncan. He killed Duncan at night, just after Duncan had knelt to say his evening prayers of confession. MacBeth relays to his wife: "They did say their prayers. One cried 'God bless us!' and 'Amen' the other, as they had seen me with these hangman's hands [about to kill them]. Listening to their fear, I could not say 'Amen,' when they did say 'God bless us!'"

"Consider it not too deeply," Lady MacBeth replies, wanting him to move on and clean the blood from his hands.

But MacBeth says in great sadness and a moment's introspection: "But wherefore could not I pronounce 'Amen'? I had most need of blessing, and 'Amen' stuck in my throat." These must be the saddest of words—a soul that can no longer speak the most simple of words of praise or acknowledgment of the grace of God.

Fundamentalism showed me the importance of words, and words have had a positive effect on my life. Fundamentalism taught me to speak clearly and forthrightly, to know what I believed and to not shy away from saying it out loud. This is one of the finest elements of fundamentalism: You own your faith. You profess it aloud. Words have meaning and power. I know that the casual ways fundamentalists have of talking about God make many people of other branches of Christianity uneasy, but I still believe that it is a spiritual gift to be treasured. It usually reflects a familiarity of a deeper sort.

But I couldn't accept for long that the meaning of everything preceded me. The final reading of all things—even God, and Scripture—must be still and always in front of us. That is how I live and talk today. However, to this day, I've never met a studied fundamentalist young person who was not well-spoken. Words matter.

if a tree falls in the woods

history and truth

*[E]verything is connected to everything else.
Therefore, life is supercharged, permeated, and
over-brimming with purpose and meaning. Most of
the time we are oblivious to it. We go about our
lives as if every event were an accident. And then
something happens and we see the connection.*
—Lawrence Kushner

When I was in third grade we moved from one suburb
west of Chicago to another. Our new neighborhood was
unincorporated and somewhat on the outskirts of town.
At the end of our road was an empty field, a space of at
least five hundred acres of original prairie that was
soon to be gobbled up by new subdivisions. In our first

year in the new house, I became accustomed to seeing pheasants there.

I'm not sure if people see pheasants in suburban Chicago much anymore, but it used to be that I would ride my bike to the end of that road, where it dead-ended into tall grasses and brush, slam on the brakes to skid my back tire around in a semi-circle to make some noise, and two or three pheasants would be scared into the air.

The pheasants were always gone within seconds of my arrival. I never saw them very clearly; the grass in the field stood higher than my head, and so I mostly just heard them, glimpsing their flapping wings and long tails ever so fleetingly. I loved to hear them squawk in fear of my noise and flounder furiously away, but I hated not seeing them in the air as they flew low out of the tall brush, slow to take flight with wings hardly strong enough to carry such heavy bodies. It was like knowing something without ever really seeing it.

The old-time paradigm for God in the world still makes sense to me; I cannot shake it. I know that we are supposed to take on a more scientific worldview in which God leaves heaven above and becomes a force in the world all about us; in which God is no longer waiting to listen like a friend or a kindly grandparent to our needs and troubles and instead becomes the power in us to meet needs and sort out troubles. But, I cannot completely do it. God is still that elusive pheasant who sees, hears, feels, and understands—without much being seen, heard, felt, or understood in return. It is really a rotten relationship in many ways: full of excitement, but also disappointments.

Christian fundamentalism began, in part, as a response to the encroachment of science into theology and other secular ideas into the church. Twelve small books were published in Chicago from 1909–12 books titled *The Fundamentals*. Some of the brightest religious leaders of the day contributed to these volumes, coining the term "fundamentalism" for their movement to take the faith back from "modernists" and liberals, emphasizing what they felt to be historically distinctive about being Christian.

There were five pillars of the original Christian fundamentalists: The miracle of the Virgin birth; the necessary sacrifice of Jesus for human sin (also known as the doctrine of the atonement); the miracle of the Resurrection; anticipation of the second coming of Christ in the end times; and, perhaps the most foundational of all, the infallibility of Scripture. The authors of *The Fundamentals* also desired to counter the liberal church's de-emphasis of the meaning and power of sin, recovering a definition of hell and heaven, and preaching the necessity of evangelism along the way. "Romanism"—the Roman Catholic Church—and "Darwinism," the new scientific paradigm, were each denounced as religions that got in the way of faith.

I still continue to live in the old paradigm of the God of creation today, but it is not because I am still a fundamentalist. The God who is a creative evolutionary force just doesn't grab me by the collar as I need to be grabbed. Also, the God who creates is beautiful, and the vertical relationship to God, rather than the horizontal dispersal of God, is a well-worn path down which I have learned how to look and find. The faith of my fathers and mothers taught me to relate to God in ways that still make sense to me. To me, it is better story, history, and passion.

While still a child, I stopped looking for that elusive presence of God. It's not that I became disappointed or felt defeated; on the contrary, God began to feel very much a part of me, inside of me. To this day, I don't know if such an idea is a beautiful reality to be celebrated or a horrible conceit. Perhaps the visions described by medieval saints like Julian of Norwich or Catherine of Siena—where God speaks private truth to an individual soul—were the same sort of thing that I felt but never gave it a name or put it into words.

I grew to have no doubts of God's existence, love, and proximity. The common sense approach of fundamentalist teaching, combined with the vividness of Christ indwelling my body, satisfied me wholly. Whatever people of other traditions kept toiling over—particularly my Catholic friends with their confessions, fasts, and requirements—seemed sad to me. If only they knew the simplicity of true faith, I thought then.

This was a time when I was struggling to sort out how I was to relate to God and the world. Both seemed all around me all of the time, and to penetrate me, and both had their appeal. As I learned to find God inside of me, and to listen for that elusive voice, I also learned in church how to avoid contact with "the world." Secular culture, we believed, had a power over people that was insidious and not to be trusted. The world was the same place that the apostle Paul had told true Christians to be wary of, and I was taught to be plenty wary, too. I believed with the earnestness of one of James Baldwin's characters in *Go Tell It on the Mountain*. "[W]hen the Lord saves you He burns out all that old Adam, He gives you a new mind and new heart, and then you don't find no pleasure in the world, you get all your joy in walking and talking with Jesus every day."

Our pastor had this as a familiar theme. "The world is crucified unto me, and I unto the world," he would say, quoting Paul. "The god of this world hath blinded the minds of them that believe not." At the time, I imagined the worlds of righteousness and unrighteousness as two concentric circles. We were at the center, besieged and surrounded by the other. Although I did not want to be blinded by evil, I found that I couldn't avoid the world, either, and it didn't always seem so evil upon contact.

In our home there were no secular music, art, and books. When I was a young child, we had our own cultural revolution, purging our lives of everything that did not serve the greater cause of God, of all that was of the world and not of God. Like a hermit who emerges from a cave for the first time in years, I had the unusual experience of discovering these things in junior high and high school, long after my friends knew they were there.

I remember once riding in the back seat of an older friend's car when I was twelve or thirteen and hearing a Bob Dylan song on the radio for the first time. It was his early acoustic stuff, recorded when he was only about twenty, vibrant and full of spit. His tone of voice and the words he sang combined to form something completely new to me. I had never really listened to music that sounded that important and yet that angry. Afraid to ask who the artist was for fear that this would mark me as oblivious, I leaned my ear back to the speaker in order to hear when the announcer said the name. The next week, I bought my first Dylan album—*The Times They are A'changin'*—and hid it from my parents. There was no one to show these things to me. There is, in fact, a long list of things I did not know and did not do. Throughout my teenage years I needed older friends to show me the way to an art museum, attend a play or a musical, even read a novel, outside of what was required in school.

I realized that the world was full of good and bad, seen and unseen. I knew supernatural things without seeing them, such as Jesus in my heart, but I also began to wonder about other supernatural things not seen. I once found some pamphlets about Catholic contemplatives, and they were referred to as the most profound of Christians. What did they do all day? I wondered. How could people in deserts, or hermitages, or nunneries have any practical value, I wondered, when, as we were taught, faith is demonstrated in good works in the world?

If a tree falls in the woods and no one is around, does it still make a sound? This familiar riddle interested me as a boy and prompted me to consider something similar but more important: If a person prays alone in the woods, or in the desert, or on the prairie, does it still matter? Does God pay attention to the prayers of the unassuming, to those without a public face of faith, to those who are quiet, and alone? The teaching I grew up with suggested that, in a spiritual sense, the tree would fall in silence, heard by no one.

Other than perfunctory petitionary prayer, meal-time graces, and prayers offered in church, the notion of deep and lasting communication with God (more than a minute or two) was completely outside of my experience. My young faith told me that the prayers of the private person wouldn't matter as much alone in the woods as they would if offered in front of a crowd of witnesses. Where the superstitions of religious ritual may be private, true faith was meant to be a public expression.

When I was eleven, I was exposed to more Catholic stories of saints through a book I discovered at the public library. It was full of tales of lengthy prayer sessions, agonizingly intense self-searching to root out unfaithfulness, days (even weeks!) of fasting, stigmata, and private visions. I didn't know what to believe. I did know that my church was involved in evangelizing Roman Catholics—believing they needed a new faith to replace the superstitions they held onto—and so I doubted (but was still compelled by sanctity in) the legends of saints.

But the question persisted: If a person prays alone in the woods, does God pay attention? I thought of my grandmother. She had no admiration for Catholic mystics that I am aware of, but she did pray every day and for a long time, and she told me that she prayed every day specifically for me. She knew Matthew, chapter 6: "[W]hen thou prayest, enter into thy closet, and when thou hast shut thy door, pray to thy Father which is in secret." I wondered: Is my life better because of my grandmother's prayers?

It is an occasional fantasy of most adolescents to leave home, at least for a time, and live in the woods or on the streets, alone. We like to dream of our autonomy when freedom seems farthest from reach. I was no different and dreamed of holing myself up in a large tree somewhere with only a few supplies and discovering the world around me without parental guidance or the instruction of adults of any kind. Jean Craighead George's wonderful book *My Side of the Mountain* was one of my favorites. Young Sam Gribley sneaks away from his suburban home and into the Catskill Mountains. "I am on my mountain in a tree home that people have passed without ever knowing that I am here," the novel begins. I used to think to myself: If I had five dollars in my pocket, how long could I make it last? What essentials would I buy and how long could I survive with only those things? I had heard of monks who live in cloisters away from the world, and I began to think of myself as something like that.

If there is a monk in the woods or in a cloister somewhere who prays every day for hours on end, who can say that God doesn't listen to him more than all of the preachers put together, I thought? Perhaps those quiet and secretive meditations are what God actually uses to guide the planet. Even now, I wonder: Is it possible that the most important human link between God and the world is a devout hermit or an elderly woman somewhere, unknown to those around them, who is praying unceasingly for all of us?

part two

all that is,
seen and unseen
my Scofield Bible

Blessed be the Lord,
who daily loadeth us with benefits,
even the God of our salvation.
—Psalm 68:19

That was one of my Grandpa Turner's favorite verses. I've quoted it from his Scofield Reference Bible, Authorized Version, 1917 edition—a battered, black book that is one of my most prized possessions. On one of the front matter pages, Grandpa wrote in blue pen: "Crow Indian Mission. Lodge Grass, Montana. Ps. 68:19." Maybe that is where he was given this particular Bible. He drew a simple scene of a Native American tipi on that page, as well, probably something that he saw in Montana. He loved the West.

He also loved that Scofield Bible. He was schooled in its system of organizing Christian history and in its conservative interpretations while in Bible college, as were my parents, and then I. It was once considered the primary study aid for any intelligent evangelical Christian. In the introduction to the 1917 edition, under which Dr. C. I. (Cyrus Ingerson) Scofield had the publishers print the straightforward instructions: "(To Be Read.)" he explains the purpose of his study aids. "In the present edition, by a new system of connected topical references, all the greater truths of the divine revelation are so traced through the entire Bible, from the place of first mention to the last, that the reader may for himself follow the gradual unfolding of these, by many inspired writers through the ages, to their culmination in Jesus Christ and the New Testament Scriptures."

Scofield's purpose was to show in as "scientific" a manner as he was able, that the Hebrew Scriptures are an elaborate, coded prelude to what comes in the Christian Testament. Scofield used the language of logic and science in an effort to show that the Bible was full of such things. He believed in what he called a "panoramic view of the Bible."

The Bible is one book. Seven great marks attest this unity. (1) From Genesis the Bible bears witness to one God. Wherever he speaks or acts he is consistent with himself, and with the total revelation concerning him. (2) The Bible forms one continuous story—the story of humanity in relation to God. (3) The Bible hazards the most unlikely predictions concerning the future, and, when the centuries have brought round the appointed time, records their fulfillment. (4) The Bible is a progressive unfolding of truth. Nothing is told all at once, and once for all. The law is, "first the blade, then the ear, after that the full corn." Without the possibility of collusion, often with centuries between, one writer of Scripture takes up an earlier revelation, adds to it, lays down the pen, and in due time another man moved by the Holy Spirit, and another, and another, add new details till the whole is complete. (5) From beginning to end the Bible testifies to one redemption. (6) From beginning to end the Bible has one great theme—the person and work of the Christ. (7) And, finally, these writers, some forty-four in number, writing through twenty centuries, have produced a perfect harmony of doctrine in progressive unfolding. This is, to every candid mind, the unanswerable proof of the divine inspiration of the Bible.

Scofield inherited his ideas from the influential British Victorian John Nelson Darby, who is known as the father of "dispensationalism." According to Darby's teachings in the 1830s, the current age, or dispensation, is ruled by Satan, and the last dispensation will be ruled by Christ, after the Second Coming. But it is Scofield's Bible that popularized the literalism and compartmentalism of dispensationalist teaching to millions of fundamentalist Christians in the twentieth century.

My own connection with Scofield's Bible came through *The Ryrie Study Bible* (1976), an updating of Scofield that my father published when he was the director of Moody Press in Chicago. Charles Ryrie taught for decades at Dallas Theological Seminary, the primary bastion of dispensationalism in America today, and he was a family friend. My Ryrie was a constant companion for several years when I was young.

Today's most visible inheritors of Scofield are Tim LaHaye and Jerry Jenkins, authors of the *Left Behind* series of novels. More than sixty million of these books have been sold so far throughout the world, topping every other bestselling author during that time. The ideas are nothing new. My grandfather preached them for half a century from his old Bible, and I learned them in Sunday school: The pre-figuring of Christ throughout the Old Testament; seven dispensations, or revelations, of God in history (innocence, conscience, human government, promise, law, grace, kingdom); each dispensation concluding with a cataclysmic event: the Fall, the Flood, the Tower of Babel, the Egyptian captivity of Israel, Christ's crucifixion, the Rapture, the Second Coming; a roadmap of coming apocalyptic events as literally interpreted from the Book of Revelation, and ways in which God tests humankind through each dispensation in order to determine the Church's faithfulness and obedience; seven years of tribulation on earth; and finally, the triumphant return of Jesus to usher in a millennium of holy rule.

In the middle 1970s, most evangelical churches in America screened the apocalyptic movie *A Thief in the Night* at least once. I saw it twice in our church basement along with hundreds of my friends and neighbors. The film opens with a terrifying scene of life on earth immediately after what is called the Rapture—that time in the future when evangelical Christians believe Christ will return in the air and call all true Christians to join him in the skies. In some translations of the Bible, it says that Christ will come in the last days "like a thief in the night." The prophecies of the enigmatic Book of Revelation say, "If therefore thou shalt not watch, I will come on thee as a thief, and thou shalt not know what hour I will come upon thee."

A Thief in the Night depicted the world trying to cope with the Rapture immediately after the first signs of it. In the opening scene of the movie, a radio announcer is heard explaining, "Millions who were living on this earth last night are not here this morning." The message of the film is clear: Do you want to be one of those left behind, or do you want to become a true Christian?

Recently, LaHaye and Jenkins have specialized in future imaginative depictions of God's testing that is to come—in that last dispensation. Scofield's Bible, in fact, with the idea of dispensations, gave birth to a whole industry of prophecy teachers and preachers and conferences throughout the world. While I was a student in Bible college I worked in the public relations office that coordinated many of these conferences. Before computers were relied on for such obvious tasks, we kept a large filing cabinet of index cards, each with the name of a church printed on it and a chronological, handwritten listing of our prophecy teachers (the ones that our department dispatched) who had preached to date from that pulpit. The cards had dates going back as far as the 1930s and 1940s.

Inspired to be one of Scofield's dispensationalists, I read many other books on the subject, including an earlier bestseller: *The Late Great Planet Earth*, by Hal Lindsey, a former boat captain in Louisiana who studied Darby and Scofield, and learned directly from Ryrie, at Dallas Theological Seminary. Hal Lindsey proclaimed the end of the world to coincide with the growth in power of Communism. The Soviet Union was the Antichrist. It all made good sense in 1970. Characteristically, wherever fundamentalist Christians found themselves and whatever our situation, we felt that our generation was undergoing the most profound challenges to spiritual fidelity ever.

My grandfathers, my parents, my Sunday school teachers, and I all believed in supernatural powers and a world to come that would surprise many of the unbelieving with its ferocity, and its justice. For us, the world to come was the most important part "of all that is, seen and unseen" in Christian faith, to use a phrase that I now recite from the Nicene Creed in church each Sunday morning.

We believe in one God,
the Father, the Almighty,

maker of heaven and earth,
of all that is, seen and unseen.

We believed that heaven and hell were as sure as death. In fact, we had greater confidence in the afterlife than we did in death because we expected that at any time Jesus could come in the air to save us from death. Your destination in the afterlife was made possible only by God's grace and that most important first decision—to become born again—that characterized the start of a fundamentalist, Christian life.

But as I look at that ancient creed again today, what is it, I wonder, that I am supposed to believe as I affirm what is "unseen," to come in the future, in faith? As a child, it was very clear, but no longer.

I have never seen much commentary on it, but the phrase always stops me in my tracks. It does not appear in the earlier, Apostles' Creed. Most likely, according to some scholars, the framers of the Nicene Creed included the notion that God is the maker "of all that is, seen and unseen" in order to counter those early heresies that taught a form of dualism where the natural world (of earth and body) is governed by evil, and the supernatural world (of heaven and spirit) is governed by God. God made it all, they wanted to emphasize—both what you see and what you cannot see.

To fulfill the divine historical road map laid out by people like Scofield and Ryrie, fundamentalists often interpret events such as wars, famines, and battles as part of the divine plan for humanity and the world.

These awful things must happen in order for the world to be ripe for the return of Jesus, we believed. But, fundamentalism also believes that there is no reason to fear the unseen future if you have made your decision for Christ, asking Jesus into your heart, and become born again. After that, the future will take care of itself, you will be safe as a member of the truly faithful, and Jesus will return to wrap up all true Christians into a divine future of divine rule.

As a child, I believed these things in step with my parents and grandparents, but I also grew to believe that the unseen future was full of other possibilities, not at all frightening or apocalyptic. Today, I believe that the future is full of opportunities for creating the sort of future that I used to only yearn for in heaven, after the end of time. The world of the unseen is the world (right here before us) of potential heaven. And the evil that we encounter is primarily what we have caused, either by our actions or by our inactions.

I believe that fundamentalism is right about one important issue, however: We cannot spiritualize the world and say that we relate to God in spirit, outside of time. We know God in time and God is in the world of history, with us. But, contrary to what my grandfathers and Scofield taught me, I don't think scriptures teach us to see danger and fear what lies ahead. So many of our fundamentalist responses seem to have roots in human anxiety and our search for definitive answers. But there is tremendous mystery in the meaning of what it means to be human together that isn't addressed by definitive answers. We are God's co-creators. In *The Sabbath*, Abraham Joshua Heschel wrote that "to [people] with God time is eternity in disguise." We are God's presence in the world, or, the eternal in time. I am no longer waiting for a day when I might escape it all in the clouds—leaving time with God—because my work is here and now.

I am glad that I was able to keep my changing beliefs hidden from my grandfathers as I grew older. By the time my Grandpa Turner died I was an Episcopalian in my late twenties working in religious book publishing for Lutherans. He never asked me about any of that, but I'll bet he was worried that I had seriously strayed, since Episcopalians and Lutherans don't usually believe in the dispensationalist approach to faith.

Soon after he died, and I had carried his casket with my brother and cousins, I went to work for a Jewish book publisher. Grandpa would have thought that working to edit and market books about Judaism made me a sort of traitor to my own faith. He wouldn't have understood. By that time, I was convinced that Scofield and Ryrie were wrong when they interpreted the covenant between God and Israel as only a temporary foreshadowing of the new covenant of Jesus. Scofield also believed—and my grandfather followed suit—that Christians should not pray the Lord's Prayer; they believed it to be a remnant of Judaism that has nothing to do with the dispensation of the new covenant. Here I was, at a Jewish publisher, praying the Lord's Prayer.

Since those days when I took all of my understanding of faith from the notes of dispensationalist study Bibles, I have come to believe that Christians and Jews should learn from each other as brothers and sisters with an equal claim on truth. But Grandpa wouldn't have liked that, either. It also would have been difficult to explain to Grandpa that I was still a Christian when I began taking retreats, praying, and studying with many other people of faith. I not only learn from my Benedictine brothers at Weston Priory in Vermont, and the Trappist monks of Our Lady of the Holy Spirit in Georgia, but also from Jews and Judaism and Muslims and Islam, our first cousins in faith. I learn from them, and I am still Christian. Grandpa wouldn't have liked that at all; he wouldn't have thought it possible, or reasonable. But this Sunday when I am affirming the Nicene Creed and praying the Lord's Prayer, I will be thinking of him.

light from light

the zeal of fundamentalist faith

Delight is to him, whom all the waves of the billows
of the seas of the boisterous mob can never shake
from this sure Keel of the Ages.
And eternal delight and deliciousness will be his,
who coming to lay him down, can say with his final
breath—O Father! . . . I have striven to be Thine,
more than to be this world's, or mine own.
—"The Sermon," from Herman Melville's *Moby-Dick*

I was a typical teenager in many ways. I had a girl-
friend; I watched sports on television with my father
and also played in the backyard and on teams; I had a
paper route and then graduated to better-paying part-
time jobs; I liked to make money and then spend it on
meaningless things; I endlessly analyzed my body in

the mirror: my hands and cheeks were chubby, eyelids too droopy, legs didn't have enough hair, and would I ever develop a respectable reason to shave?

In this adolescent, normal hormonal funk, I also developed tremendous certainty in spiritual matters. You wouldn't have known it to look at me, but I knew everything. Faith may have been "the substance of things hoped for, the evidence of things not seen" for the writer of Hebrews, but for me at age fourteen it was the assurance of things convinced of, the conviction of things well-argued.

Fundamentalism taught me to know what I believed, and to help others in finding the same certainty. We believed that it was possible, and common, to convince doubters of the truths, as we called them, of faith. I had no experience doing some of the things that it seems (from the New Testament) disciples of Jesus might do: I never cured the sick, raised the dead, made lepers clean again, or cast out demons, spoke in mystical languages, or experienced special visions. It isn't that I tried and failed; I never tried. But I knew the fundamentals of faith.

My hero was Josh McDowell. His book *Evidence that Demands a Verdict* became my encyclopedia. He taught me that "Christianity appeals to history, the facts of history," and quoting another popular evangelical teacher, Clark Pinnock, McDowell explained in his public lectures and in his books that "The facts backing the Christian claim are not a special kind of religious fact. They are the cognitive, informational facts upon which all historical, legal, and ordinary decisions are based."

For the zealous, evangelical teenager (and that probably summarizes McDowell's target market), apologetics became our brand of what we called "spiritual warfare"—the battle between good and evil. Quoting Scripture, we talked about "put[ting] on the whole armor of God," which meant, for us, that we would not be wounded by the rejections or criticisms of the enemy—unbelievers. Apologetics, a/k/a the logical defense of the faith, was ideally suited to our need to know, a ready set of answers to an equally ready set of questions: How do you know that God exists? Did Jesus really rise from the dead three days after his crucifixion? Is there life after death? We were equipped, to use the biblical word for it, with right doctrine in order to counter various religious groups (Mormons, Jehovah's Witnesses, Roman Catholics), cults, the teachings of evolution and the New Age and everyday, common doubt.

Spiritual warfare, a/k/a "our struggle . . . against rulers, against authorities, against cosmic powers of this present darkness, against the spiritual forces of evil in the heavenly places," not only was a felt presence in our lives but it had a face in each doubter that we confronted. We believed that a logical debate of the issues of faith and doubt was one powerful way to combat the forces of evil.

I relished taking on my friends at school. Like Josh McDowell, I tried to be sharp, witty, and funny, while I buried them in facts and scriptures. I followed the apologist's advice and memorized key verses and the essential points to overcome all of the most common objections. Occasionally, the arguments were spirited, as when I tried to convince Catholic friends that veneration of saints and the Virgin Mary was empty superstition, or when I tried to convince an atheist friend that the eyewitness reports in the New Testament were reliable historical evidence of Christ's resurrection. But the results were never what I hoped they would be. No minds were changed, let alone "souls saved," which was always the goal.

I also argued with my fellow fundamentalists. It was sport that mattered. We enjoyed the minutiae of fundamentalist doctrine: Will the Rapture come before the thousand years of testing prophesied in the Book of Revelation, or after? Are supernatural "gifts" of the Spirit—such as speaking in tongues (uttering sounds in unknown languages, as the first Christians did on the day of Pentecost, according to the Book of Acts)— a means of prophecy, meaningless babbling, or actions of the devil? On the subject of this last question, I even did some firsthand research. While visiting our neighborhood Assemblies of God church I was encouraged one evening to learn to speak in tongues. Later, back at my home church, my pastor described this experience of mine as further evidence that speaking in tongues was never a genuine gift of the Spirit, since they were busy trying to teach kids to do it at the Assemblies of God church. So when I returned to the Assemblies church once again, with a friend one Sunday evening, I felt like an undercover cop seeking to make a bust.

We held no real value for doubt in a spiritual life. It was something to be removed, a stain that could be cleaned up. Doubt was clearly a weakness. As Josh McDowell liked to say: "Unbelief requires a lot of denial on your part. To disbelieve all of the evidences of the Christian faith is to put your head in the sand." The unbeliever was like the coward who refuses to sign up for military duty even though the threat is imminent and real.

This doesn't mean, however, that faith, for me at that time, took on greater spiritual meaning in doubt's absence. Fundamentalist faith rarely carried with it the sheen of newness that comes with conversion. Faith was a commitment, an act of will, and we set out to strengthen our wills. Throughout my fundamentalist experience, my faith had much more will than it had spirit.

Love was similar: like faith, true love was something willed, not felt. God was not interested (or perhaps in control) of how you felt, we believed, but God was very much at work in your will. To this day, I think that the nature of our relationship with God becomes our most important model for our loving, human relationships. I met my wife, Danelle, at age twenty, and my love—like my faith—had much more to do with will than spirit. Slowly, over the almost twenty years since, as I've learned to know God in spirit and not just in truth, I've also learned more fully how to love with spirit.

Confidence was doubt's antidote, the outcome of a healthy faith. As a young teenager, I was already learning it. I was taught that with greater confidence comes deeper faith. So I studied the expressions, the subjects, the look of confident faith. It is no accident that leaders in certain religious communities or traditions give a uniform impression when you meet them. It is schooled.

During my senior year at Wheaton Christian High School, I and an equally earnest friend petitioned the school principal for permission to lead a chapel service. Chapel was compulsory for all and an integral part of student life, but it usually featured guest speakers: clergy or the school chaplain.

David and I had been convicted by the Holy Spirit of spiritual laziness—we felt this spiritual challenge genuinely and profoundly—but, as other students didn't seem to have been likewise challenged by God, we believed that we would start a revival on campus. We believed that a demonstration of the passion of Christ would bring any audience to its knees. David researched the sequence of events that brought Jesus to Calvary, while I studied the tools that were used by the Romans to torture him. We stood behind the pulpit that morning and recounted the blows, the whipping and tearing of flesh, the probable length and thickness and blunt effect of the nails on bone, and the way in which the lynching of crucifixion brought on a slow suffocation.

I can only imagine now how our classmates must have despised us. But, zealots can be useful and, to my surprise, my potential to become a zealot was soon recognized by our pastor. He asked me to serve on the planning committee for a series of evangelistic rallies to be hosted by our church the following year. Such tent meetings—although uncommon by the early 1980s—still represented the pinnacle of the public face of fundamentalism. They indicated our desire to tap into what was a golden age of evangelism, when Billy Sunday and then the young Billy Graham stormed the United States preaching repentance, ushering thousands of souls into the kingdom of God.

I no longer want to be an evangelist, but I still hold onto the robust feeling I had in evangelistic meetings— that the Spirit of God is moving among us, in us, in me. I still believe that God's Spirit is unleashed in the world and at work in each of our souls. Fundamentalism taught me that it is possible to stir the soul, to rouse our affections, conscience, emotions, will, and intellect by an earnest approach to matters of faith. There is nothing wrong with preaching it from the rooftops. Fundamentalism showed me how authentic it can be to express your faith earnestly and genuinely, wanting to help others with what has helped you. I only wish that my fundamentalist friends and family would welcome other, competing, voices on the rooftops. I would rather hear from all people of faith how God is at work.

I knew that my grandparents and my parents were proud of my zeal for evangelism. My Grandpa and Grandma Sweeney may have been the most proud of all. "Your grandfather always wished that one of his sons would have become a preacher, I think," Grandma once told me. "Of course, he has always been proud of his sons' work—and they are all involved in full-time Christian ministry of some kind—but I think he is so proud of you in your desire to preach." That stirred my soul. How I wanted to be what they believed I should be!

There is another evocative phrase from the Nicene Creed—"Light from Light"—that explains how Christ emanates from God the Father:

> We believe in one Lord, Jesus Christ,
> the only Son of God,
> eternally begotten of the Father,
> God from God, Light from Light. . . .

In late antiquity when the Creed was drawn up, every educated person *knew* with certainty that the sun's light was not only constantly there, but the effect of the sun's light was instantaneous on the surface of the earth. (The concept of light taking time to travel was not clarified until the Danish scientist Olaf Roemer conducted experiments with the moons of Jupiter in 1676.) The constancy and instantaneousness of God and Christ is probably the primary metaphor that the authors of the Creed intended with the phrase "Light from Light." Christ, the eternal Logos, is of the same light as the Father, both in time and space.

I wished to be of the same light as that of my father and mother. I wanted to be another link in the constant and continuous chain of faith. I wished to link myself to what they had become and what they wanted for me, and zeal for apologetics carried me far. The light of their faith shone brightly and glowed beautifully. I was never more proud than when I was spiritually what they wanted me to be. In the end, though, it was impossible to bridge the gap between their light and my own.

I still remember the fervor of faith that sustained me in fundamentalism. It is difficult to have that sort of passion, I think, without religious imperatives. Great saints live with very little doubt. I live by far fewer imperatives, now, and I am probably correspondingly less faithful.

eight

begotten not made

arguing with a spiritual inheritance

I'm not impressed with the outfit of a tightrope walker until I see what he can do in it.
—Ludwig Wittgenstein

Before class began I could tell that this was no ordinary class. For one thing, there were no required textbooks marked on the list in the campus bookstore. In place of a list of titles to purchase, it read: "See Instructor." That was strange. Also, the course description did not mention any typical requirements, no term papers or quizzes. "Weekly reports" is all it read. This was a required course for all new students, but the teacher was referred to everywhere as an instructor, not a professor. It was Evangelism 101. My first Monday morning of my first semester at Moody Bible Institute.

I was on time. Two upperclassmen were at the front of the room when I arrived. They were sitting atop the instructor's desk, talking with some other new freshmen, fielding questions about the school and student life. One of them was quite short, Chinese-American, and his friend, the taller one, was lanky and talkative. I had seen them for the first time on move-in day four days earlier. They shared a room on my dormitory floor and had told me that some of my Dylan records were of questionable taste. "You don't want to take your mind off of what you are really here for," the shorter one had said. It turns out they were the instructor's student assistants for Evangelism 101—star pupils.

The instructor arrived about ten minutes late. He was a squat man, built like a farmer, late middle-aged, with thick, black-frame glasses. He had a blue-collar reputation on campus; unlike the handsome and smooth evangelists who taught would-be preachers, Mr. Estes was a street-worker. His work was done far from pulpits and blackboards.

He began to lay the groundwork for our sixteen weeks of course work: "You are accustomed to academic study, I know that. But, this is much different," he began. "In this class, you will learn how to save souls, and you will practice a variety of techniques in order to succeed. We will discuss apologetics— the logical defense of the faith—so that you can give the most intelligent answers to people's questions, but your real work will be on the street, not in books."

I was squirming in my seat. Just a few months before arriving at Bible college I had served on that evangelism committee at our home church. I had helped to organize an old-fashioned tent meeting, inviting a renowned evangelist to come to town and preach for the week. But, this was different. Despite years of informal training, one-on-one witnessing still unnerved me. I had never really done it, or at least, not as an adult talking to other adults. That summer I had been reading Henry David Thoreau's *Journal* at the urging of a friend, and had copied down the line, "The inexpressible privacy of a life—how silent and unambitious it is." I was thinking on that as my new instructor continued.

"You must witness one-on-one to at least two people each week," he said. "Your weekly reports will tell me how you are doing. And, I will meet with each of you twice each month to discuss your progress, concerns, whatever comes up. This is what it's all about, everyone; this is why you are all here."

That evening in the cafeteria, the student assistants from Evangelism 101 sat down at my dinner table. They may have noticed the reaction on my face earlier in class.

"Do you want to hear a great witnessing technique?" the tall one asked.

"Sure," I said.

"Now, follow this," began the short one. "The two of us board the Michigan Avenue bus at rush hour—the one that is an express and doesn't stop for about twenty blocks. We act as if we don't know each other and we take seats next to other passengers, me in the seat directly in front of him." He pointed at his friend.

The tall one went on: "After a couple of blocks, I lean forward with my Bible in hand and ask the person sitting next to him, 'Have you ever read the Gospels? I was just reading this really cool thing about Jesus . . . .'

"And then, I immediately speak up and sound interested, even though he wasn't talking directly to me. And . . . a conversation begins," said the short guy, winking at his partner.

"We've saved seven souls that way in the past eight months."

I had no similar luck or creativity, but I dove right in. I witnessed to everybody, it seemed, and couldn't save a single soul. From the drunks at night on Rush Street: "Whatch you talkin' bout? I luhhvv Jee-sus!" to the manager at Mr. G's, the hamburger joint parodied by John Belushi and Dan Ackroyd on *Saturday Night Live*: "Never mind! Keep moving! Next!!" I witnessed on the train, on the bus, on the street, and in a cab. I was like a character in a Dr. Seuss story: Will you witness on the train? Will you witness on the bus? Will you witness on the street? You must, you must!

My weekly reports were colorful, full of minute detail, but short on results. My instructor was patient. I once wrote: "I am enjoying the lively conversations with people—seven in this past week alone, each averaging about five to ten minutes—but I cannot seem to get people to make a *decision*." The instructor suggested that perhaps I was targeting the wrong people.

"I don't think that you are allowing the Spirit to guide you when you are out there," he said. "Pray, and listen."

I did as he said, but God was very quiet. Over the course of the second half of the term, I began focusing on people of other religious traditions—by that I mean those people whom I thought I could visibly identify as belonging to other faiths.

On the train one day I approached a group of three young men with shaved heads wearing beautiful, long robes. "Did you know that Jesus died for you?" I asked them.

"Of course," one of them said, "Hare Krishna." They smiled and I smiled back, completely confused.

Another time, I happened upon two older Muslim men at midday prayer. It was a sunny day in Daley Plaza as I watched them roll out their prayer rugs in a quiet corner of the square. They were window-washers on break. I watched them praying for a few minutes, standing, prostrating, chanting. Then, I approached.

"May I talk with you for a few minutes?" I said, holding my Bible in plain view. They prostrated again, kissing the front of their mats at the same time. They may not have heard me. I cleared my throat.

"Excuse me," I said. But then I stopped.

I'll never forget the look on their faces. They paused just long enough to shoot me a quick glance of simultaneous contempt and bewilderment, then returned their attention to prayer. I moved along, sheepishly, looking just once over my shoulder to see the two men on their knees holding their hands in front of their faces, eyes tightly shut. The beautiful pitch of their soft chants rang in my ears all the way home.

Somehow I ended up with a "B" in Evangelism 101, perhaps just to honor my effort—but I never successfully saved anyone.

Witnessing was only one part of my required spiritual work in Bible college. I was also assigned to teach a weekly Sunday school class of high school kids at a church in a working-class Polish neighborhood on the northwest side of the city. St. Hyacinth Church was not far from the corner of Foster and Kedzie. I took the L train to get there each Sunday morning accompanied by two other students, both girls, whose job it was to sing in the choir.

Each Sunday, after an early breakfast, I would meet the girls in the quad. We had two trains and a bus to take to our stop on Foster Avenue, and we would walk a short distance through the neighborhood to the church from there. I cannot imagine how early those girls must have woken up in order to make themselves up the way that they did each Sunday morning, but it was really something to see. Big hair with curls and bows; floral-patterned dresses to the ankles; sashes; tall, laced boots or high heels; eye-liner and blush and lipstick; and a fat study Bible complete with embroidered Bible-cover cradled in each of their arms like an infant. Stepping off campus and onto the streets of Chicago was scary business for me in their company.

There aren't many people who ride subway or elevated trains on Sunday mornings, and those who do are not usually headed to worship services. It is a miracle that we never got mugged.

I wanted to make smart Christians out of those kids. We studied the Bible, and memorized parts of it, applying the weekly lessons to daily life. My lesson plans included commentaries on texts, atlases of Bible lands, and inspirational thoughts from preachers and teachers of the past. I don't know how relevant it all sounded to sixteen-year-olds living on the northwest side.

I grew up in one of those religious environments where knowing what you believe is both a hobby and your duty—the way that West Bank Israeli settlers must know their automatic rifles, or the way that enthusiastic tax lawyers know the tax code. The Bible was, for us, full of doctrines and stories with morals at the end of them. Logistically, we put it on as the armor of God and used it to take on the world. Devotionally, it was a sieve through which we poured our lives. A "storehouse of facts," nineteenth-century theologian Charles Hodge called the Bible, and that is how we used it. The test that you believed something was that you said so. I taught my Sunday school students to say so, just like me. It was transmitted wisdom, and after a while, it began to leave me feeling cold. I began to wonder how I had become so certain. I knew the right answers to a lot of questions, but I began to wonder what questions I didn't know, yet.

By the end of my first year at Moody, I found myself in an unusual predicament, as I struggled with feelings of wanting to step outside of all that I knew. I knew that where I was, and who I was trying to be, was somehow not my identity. The faith of my fathers no longer felt like it fit. The Austrian philosopher Ludwig Wittgenstein once remarked, "A person will be imprisoned in a room with a door that's unlocked and opens inwards as long as it does not occur to him to pull rather than to push it." By this time in my life, I knew that the door of faith was unlocked, but I had more work to do before I could see clearly to pull rather than push.

■ ■ ■ ■ ■ ■ ■ nine

one holy catholic and apostolic church

coming to terms with the sheep and the goats

The summer after my year in Bible college, I was sent by the Conservative Baptist Foreign Missionary Society as a missionary to Southeast Asia. Many weekends of the previous twelve months were spent raising money for my journey: Writing letters to relatives, talking to groups of church leaders, and speaking before my home church, prompting the congregation to take a special collection toward the expenses of my trip. My job title was assistant church planter, in the language of the Missionary Society, and they sent me to Batangas City, in the province of Batangas, at the southern edge of the island of Luzon, Philippines.

I arrived in Manila, the capital city of the Philippines, at the end of a very long day. My flight pattern had taken me from Chicago to Minneapolis-St. Paul, to Seattle, to Seoul, to Taiwan, where we deplaned and sat in a hot holding room for about two hours, before finally making our way into Manila.

The capital city was exuberant when I arrived in June of 1986. The dictatorship of Ferdinand and Imelda Marcos had come to an abrupt and nonviolent end only four months earlier in the most remarkable political development in the country's short history. Corazon Aquino, the widow of slain opposition leader Benigno Aquino, had rallied millions of Filipinos in protest of the corrupt Marcos government, calling an end to it, and taking the name "People Power" for the movement. Three years after her husband's murder Corazon Aquino became president of the Philippines, and the Marcoses were living in exile in the United States.

My aunt and uncle, also missionaries in the Philippines, met me at the airport in Manila. The terminal was loud, brightly lit, and crawling with people as I walked down the ramp into the waiting area where people waited for loved ones and friends. I could barely hear my aunt as she called out instructions as to where we could find my luggage and where we would go to find the car. As we drove out of Manila that afternoon—where a steady honking of the car horn is the only key to survival—I sat in the backseat with many doubts. How was I supposed to lead a youth group—something I had never done before—of kids from another country?

Was I, at eighteen, prepared to teach the Bible to anyone, let alone to new, adult Christian converts?

It was hot. The dry season was still in full force, and I was glad to have bought a few new, cheap, cotton short-sleeve shirts at TJ Maxx the week before leaving Chicago. I wouldn't see rain until near the end of my stay, late in August, and we all ran outside at the first sound of it to dance in the front yard.

Within days of my arrival, the people of Batangas City were celebrating one of their many festivals, parading up and down the streets of town dressed in bright colors, yelling and singing with joy, and carrying Santo Niños above their heads. The Santo Niño (literally, "Holy Child"), is the most common religious symbol of the Philippines. Santo Niños are found everywhere throughout the country: hanging from rearview mirrors of jeepneys (open-air bus-like taxis), as stickers on children's school notebooks, mini-statues, and more. The Niño is usually European in appearance, complete with blonde curls, which looks out of place in a land of dark brown eyes and brown hair. These Child Jesuses are each made in the style of the one first presented by the Portuguese explorer Ferdinand Magellan to local Queen Juana upon his landing on the islands in 1521. Magellan traveled under the flag of Spain and so claimed the land for King Philip of Spain, hence the name, the Philippines.

I had been sent by the Missionary Society with the goal of converting Catholics into Baptists. The Roman Catholic Church is a powerful force in everyday life in the Philippines. In the center of Batangas City was the Basilica of the Immaculate Conception, built in 1857, and decreed by Pope Pius XII in 1946 (just after the Americans liberated the islands from Japanese occupation) to be a *basilica minor* of the Church in the East, the only one of its kind in the country. Most of the churches are full of people for Mass each week, but we were across town in a rented hall with fifteen to twenty people talking about our version of Jesus.

We believed that Filipino Catholics needed to convert to what we considered true Christianity if they wanted to be saved. We taught that the sacraments of the Church, such as taking communion, going to confession, and doing penance, would not bring either happiness or security, on earth or in heaven. We preached that each person must confess his or her sins (including the sin of being duped by the Catholic Church for so long), and publicly profess new, born-again faith in Jesus Christ. Then, each must be re-baptized, or, baptized correctly.

Nearly every Catholic who grows up in the faith is baptized as a child. They are "sprinkled" with the water, as we liked to differentiate, during the baptism ceremony as infants, rather than "immersed" in it, as we believed the Scriptures taught it should be done. We also taught the necessity of an adult decision to be baptized. You had to know what you were doing; the verbal commitment was the test of truth.

Just as the first Baptists who grew out of the reforms of the Protestant Reformation in the sixteenth century set out to re-baptize Catholics, so we taught that a proper baptism was the most important early sign that salvation was genuine. It was the litmus test of faithfulness; it demonstrated that the faith of Christ had taken hold inside. After all, Christ had said to the first apostles: "Go ye therefore, and teach all nations, baptizing them in the name of the Father, and of the Son, and of the Holy Ghost: Teaching them to observe all things whatsoever I have commanded you: and, lo, I am with you alway, *even* unto the end of the world."

Our targets for conversions were Roman Catholic married men who had standing in the community. As I learned in Bible college, evangelizing had a plan attached to it. We knew that such men would likely bring with them their wives, their children, and perhaps some extended family. Many of them owned local businesses, or were leaders in the provincial government. So, once they expressed interest in learning more about us and our new church, we remained in close contact with them throughout the week to be sure that they came to church on Sunday morning. We visited their homes and led Bible studies. We socialized with them, as we were often invited to be special, honored guests at birthday parties. We wooed them.

Our house was beautiful, only a few blocks from the *basilica minor*, in a new subdivision of homes for the wealthy. Around the perimeter of the property there was a protective, high, stone wall that had shards of glass poking out from along the top. We had a full-time housekeeper. The house and trappings, too, were part of the missionary strategy. Our aim was to identify with the upper crust and the influential in order to show that coming over to our side was a step in the right direction.

Families in a Catholic country like the Philippines are asked to do nothing less than denounce their tradition, their parents, their extended family, and what their country and community stand for. Conversion is not casual, as it is in the New World. It means changing everything; it means saying out loud to your friends and family and neighbors: "Our tradition is wrong. The ways in which our family has believed and worshiped for as long as we can remember, are wrong."

The pain of some of these families, as they struggled—weighing the relative merits of eternal salvation (as we saw it) versus everything that they knew and loved (their families, their communities, their church)—struck me deeply. Before I left the States, I did not understand the difference between *saving* souls, which I knew I needed to do, and *caring* for souls, which I had not learned how to do.

It is no wonder to me now that we had very little real success in our work in Batangas. We taught the people with whom we came in contact how to talk about God in ways that brought piety into everyday life, and I think that we offered most of them an understanding of the Bible for the first time in their lives, but in the end, we measured success by souls saved, and there were few, according to our standards of measurement. Nevertheless, we comforted ourselves by comparing our results to those of biblical prophets who toiled for years without numerical success. Noah warned his neighbors for decades while building the boat and, in the end, had only his extended family on board. We were planting seeds, we told ourselves, and we honestly believed it.

By the time that my summer was over, I was convinced that what we were doing was wrong in its disregard for the life, community, culture, and the faith of the people that we had come to help. I came face to face with a series of real, human examples of how the faith of my childhood might hurt others. Was the kingdom of God really so divisive? Were the sheep and goats really the Baptists and the Catholics, as I had grown up thinking? I didn't think so. My missionary experience became for me a case study of how truth is not as simple as I had been told it was.

Protest is at the heart of fundamentalist faith. Fundamentalists are the most rigorously self-examining people that I know, and they can also be the most critical of the structures, organizations, and situations around them. I still regard these as positive traits in any person: To know what you believe and to be able to articulate what you don't agree with, as well. At the heart of this spirit of critique is the necessity of finding one's authentic, spiritual self. I was beginning to see that my authentic self lay outside of the boundaries of fundamentalist faith. I felt angry, a sort of flagrant denial, toward some of the ideas that I had previously held dear (such as the need to evangelize Catholics), at this time in my life. For some people—for me at least—this sort of wrestling is a necessary step on their spiritual journey.

■ ■ ■ ■ ■ ■ ■ ten

the life of the world to come

listening for the will of God

Our everyday words sometimes deceive us. We change clothes, change lanes, change seats. Subject-verb-predicate. But, you don't change faith like you change clothes. We do not put on faith without time and effort as easily as can put words together, and similarly, we don't shed it easily.

Abandoning faith was never an option for me. I couldn't have done it if I had tried. Deep inside of me, questioning and then, ultimately, leaving my fundamentalist faith was not simply a casual subject for debate, but a matter of my life and death. One of the great preachers of my grandfathers' generation was Dr. John R. Rice, founder of the Sword of the Lord Foundation in Murfreesboro, Tennessee. In one of his many books, Dr. Rice explained that, "Not to win souls is the sin of blood-guilt, the sin of soul-manslaughter." "O Christian," he wrote, "is there blood on your hands? Are you guilty of the death of immortal souls for whom Christ died, because you did not warn them? . . . [I]f you do not win souls, you are not right with God. . . . If you follow the Saviour at all, you follow afar off." I sure didn't want that to be me.

But the souls before me no longer looked so desperate. I was no longer convinced that they were in fact dying. I was no longer faced with a sea of souls needing the stamp of right faith and the proper exclamation of it. When I was a child in a crowd of people I never felt connected to those around me; instead, I saw only faces of lost souls. At this time in my life, after my summer in the Philippines, I began to feel different in crowds. I was sometimes able to see Christ in others. I began to see people within their own traditions and cultures, often living devout lives on different religious paths, forms of spiritual life not to be argued with.

In addition to cultivating these doubts about the theology I was schooled in, I also became skeptical about the goals I had set before me. Up to that point, it had been clear that God wanted me to become a preacher, an evangelist, or an apologist of some sort. That was what I had felt was God's will for me, and it's all that I had imagined for myself.

God's will is such a momentous concept—one of the more remarkable subjects dreamed up by the human imagination. Before Christ, Aristotle wrote that God was like an Unmoved Mover, the only thing in the universe that relies on nothing else for its existence. The stars and heavenly bodies, us and the earth itself, all move because we are caused to move by the Unmoved Mover. God, then, has plenty of will, but God's will is almost completely undiscoverable. Such a distant God is far from the personal God of the Jewish people, the God that we adopted as Christians.

Jesus spoke often about the will of the Father, sometimes as if he knew it well, and on other occasions as if he was working to fulfill it, and occasionally with some struggling to understand it. Jesus taught us to pray with him to God: "Thy kingdom come. Thy will be done in earth, as it is in heaven." He said: "For whosoever shall do the will of my Father which is in heaven, the same is my brother, and sister, and mother." Jesus absolved God from the ultimate responsibility of the death of sinners when he explained, "[I]t is not the will of your Father which is in heaven, that one of these little ones should perish." Then there are those famous words of Jesus prayed in the Garden of Gethsemane before his arrest: "Father, if thou be willing, remove this cup from me: nevertheless, not my will, but thine, be done." Finally, there are many verses in John's Gospel that have stirred controversies over the centuries as they inspire some to think that Jesus was not fully God, because of how he spoke about God's will. "Jesus saith unto them, My meat [or, true sustenance] is to do the will of him that sent me, and to finish his work."

As fundamentalists, we "discerned" God's will as a matter of course. Without any outside jury, priest, or interpretation, we simply matched our talents or "spiritual gifts," in theological language, with one of the truly God-soaked professions, and the image of a valuable Christian life would soon become clear. All that was then needed was the gradual emergence of success in order to confirm God's will for your life. If I showed the signs of a successful leader and teacher I must be on the correct path.

But as I gradually realized, not all of my desires and talents had applications that were understood by my family and church as reflecting the true will of God. Some of my interests and passions soon failed to pass the test of God's ready approval, particularly when they concerned political issues that were at odds with the majority opinion at Bible college, at my kitchen table at home, or in my home church. When I spoke my heart, I began to hear: "That's not what God would want."

While on spring break in Florida with one of my friends, I sat up alone late one night glued to the television as American planes bombed downtown Tripoli and felt the complicity of the deaths that resulted there. I also felt the immediacy of fear and dread that I might one day be called on to do the bombing. "If it is God's will, it will happen," pastor said. But I became interested in the peace movement, in the ideas of both secular and religious leaders urging nuclear disarmament in the United States and the Soviet Union. I read books and signed petitions and couldn't understand why our pastor thought it was God's will that the United States military attacked targets in Libya in the spring of 1986.

Several months earlier, I had received government papers in the mail requiring me to register for the Selective Service. So if the draft were ever to be instituted again, they wanted to know where to find me. My reading of the Gospels had begun to convince me (even though it wasn't part of the curriculum at Moody) that pacifism made sense. I also became convinced that nonviolence was the true way of Christ. Soon, I felt alone, needing support for a changing vision of the will of God.

I reached out to a nearby Mennonite counseling center with my questions about registering for the Selective Service. They showed me how to fill out the form as required, but also how to register my intent not to comply. I hand-wrote on the form, "I am a Conscientious Objector (CO)," because there was no such option or category provided. Then I followed up the form with personal letters addressed to my congressmen and senators, making my intentions of conscience clear. A Mennonite pastor taught me to keep these documents in a file, and how to prepare a defense of my sincerity, if the need should ever arise.

My upbringing in the church taught me that if I was doing something I felt was right, there might be conflict. I am thankful that fundamentalism taught me not to shy away from conflict of conscience, and spirit.

During my second semester in Bible college, I wrote a paper for one of my classes in which I praised two contemporary, nonviolent world governments inspired by Mahatma Gandhi's teachings and example. Gandhi's *Autobiography* influenced me deeply. I focused on the prime minister of New Zealand, David Lange, and his refusal to allow nuclear warships, even those of allies such as the United States, into New Zealand territorial waters, and on the People Power movement of Corazon Aquino and others in the Philippines.

None of my idealism made much sense to my family or my teachers. God's will had already been figured out—calculated in minute detail. We were in the midst of the second to last dispensation of God, a time just prior to the Rapture of true Christians before a seven-year period of tribulation. In other words, according to the dispensationalist system, wars and calamities were to be expected. They were God's will. To work for or to desire social change was considered a secular concern. Spiritual change, on the other hand, is miraculous, complete. I again became suspect in the minds of friends and family when I started describing Jesus as a man of tolerance, selflessness, and peace, because I sounded like Christian liberals who say similar things. In our fundamentalist view, Christ was about sudden, history-altering, world-shattering change.

I began to read beyond the syllabus in those last weeks of Bible college. It amazed me that such a thing as historical and textual criticism of the Bible even existed. I had never been told about them. "You mean to tell me that the Gospels of Matthew and Luke may not have been written by the friends of Jesus, and that they may have, in fact, been written two generations after Christ's death?" I once exclaimed to a professor. Similarly, I reported one day to my father: "There are devout Christians who do not believe in the Flood or the Creation as history." It was as if I had discovered that my childhood home and church and everything that I knew did not actually sit on sturdy land, but on the back of an enormous turtle, and the turtle kept moving underneath me.

In the Philippines, while teaching a weekly Bible study on the letter of Paul to the Ephesians, I became more interested in the home altar in the living room of my hosts than in what the commentaries had to say about the next chapter of Paul's letter. Before and after our study twice each week—in a quiet living room where the rest of the large, extended family stayed in the back rooms so as to avoid contact with me—I asked my friends about the images of saints, small statuettes, and brilliantly colored Virgin Marys that adorned the set-aside space at the center of the room. I knew that these things were supposed to be idols, but they drew me in with their gazes and their simplicity. I was supposed to teach these young Christians—a brother and sister who were both professionals, a high school teacher and a nurse—that these devotional objects should be smashed on a rock outside, or melted like the golden calf of the ancient Israelites, but I couldn't.

I also grew to admire the way that my Filipino friends subtly and graciously subverted our missionary work. While they were grateful that we brought the Bible into their homes, making it accessible to them for the first time, and we showed them how to talk about God in ways that make spirituality a more natural part of life, they rejected the radical faith that we required, always with tremendous kindness. At Bible study, or at dinner in their homes they would apologize and explain that they still attended Catholic services with their families.

But most important at this time, spiritual practice showed me that there was more to the spiritual life than had previously met my eye. I became interested in different types of prayer and meditation and began to experience a different sort of relationship with God, in Christ, than I had previously known.

My daily prayer times slowly became longer and more and more quiet. I found that I had less and less to say, less to argue about than I had before. I began to understand that I had a spiritual identity, that it was nuanced, unique, and that everyone else had one, too. There is a quiet, singular truth in each one of us. This truth has as much to do with God's love, experienced in friendship with Christ, as it does with God's sacrifice, experienced through the lordship of Christ.

Carl Sandburg, the strange poet of my home state of Illinois, wrote a poem called "To Billy Sunday" in 1915. He screamed at the fiery evangelist known for his showmanship in words that began to stir something inside of me, both anger and a desire for a peaceful or at-peace faith:

You come along . . . tearing your shirt . . . yelling about Jesus.

I want to know . . . what the hell . . . you
know about Jesus.

Jesus had a way of talking softly and everybody
except a few bankers and higher-ups among the
con men of Jerusalem liked to have this Jesus
around because he never made any fake passes
and everything he said went and he helped the
sick and gave the people hope.

I began to feel like the foil of Sandburg's poem, a con
man who didn't really know Jesus.

This Jesus guy was good to look at, smelled good,
listened good. He threw out something fresh
and beautiful from the skin of his body and the
touch of his hands wherever he passed along.

I wanted to be sure that I really knew Jesus. I had
always been told that Jesus was mine, but knowing
God's will for how to be his, was changing for me. It
was during my summer in the Philippines that I began
to experience something of divine love, the "fresh and
beautiful" side of Jesus that Carl Sandburg wrote about.
Just as I was helping my Filipino friends experience the
God of the Bible for the first time, the complexity,
celebrations, and joy of their spiritual lives began to
open my mind and heart to experience a love of God
that was lively, mutable, and intimate. Changing faith
began to feel less like rejecting and more like accepting.

We still need to save souls; human beings are lost without a relationship to God. Fundamentalism taught me that much. We all need saving—again and again—from greed, hate, selfishness, and all of the other vices that consume us, keeping us far from experiencing and understanding the love of God. But, we also need wider hearts and wider experiences of new life, new birth, and the love of God. The formula was not as simple as I was led to believe.

In 1735, Jonathan Edwards, the fiery American revivalist preacher who made famous the unfortunate phrase "Sinners in the Hands of an Angry God" as one of his sermon titles, once quoted in one of his sermons a passage from the Song of Songs traditionally called "The Bride's Reverie": "By night on my bed I sought him whom my soul loveth: I sought him, but I found him not. I will rise now, and go about the city in the streets, and in the broad ways I will seek him whom my soul loveth: I sought him, but I found him not." This sort of devotion and yearning for the divine embrace, experienced in the heart, was something compelling for me, and in the religion I knew, seemed so dim.

part three

eleven

I should have been too saved

discovering new fundamentals

I should have been too saved—I see—
Too rescued—Fear too dim to me
That I could spell the Prayer
I knew so perfect—yesterday—
—Emily Dickinson

Part One of this memoir might have been titled "Saved Too Little," and this part could then be titled "Saved Too Much." As a child, I always wanted to be more saved, or at least, more sure that I was in the right. I strove hard to be born again and again and again. But after my missionary experience and after leaving Bible college, I felt overdone, needing to strip away a few layers.

There are good reasons why the Buddhists talk so much about trying to hold onto a "beginner's mind," a spirit of ever-freshness and naiveté before God. Jesus emphasized to his followers that it is the simple faith of a child that is the surest path to heaven. Religious experience, both positive and negative, easily slides into dissatisfaction without guidance or counsel to help make sense of it.

One of the authors that my Mennonite mentors introduced me to at age eighteen was the monk Thomas Merton. I was first drawn to his teachings on nonviolence, essays and letters written against the Vietnam War and the threatened use of nuclear weapons. Merton published many of these pieces clandestinely in the 1960s, sending mimeographed pages off to friends, because his superiors told him that bishops should comment on such things, not contemplatives.

Merton was always gregarious. While an undergraduate at Columbia University, he drew cartoons for the school paper, visited nightclubs, hung out in Greenwich Village, had many girlfriends at parties, and dabbled in mysticism. By the time he made his way to The Abbey of Gethsemani in rural Kentucky—after stints of joining the Catholic Worker movement, teaching English at a small college in New York State, writing a bad novel, and an unsuccessful attempt at becoming a Franciscan—he had many friends and ambitions and a lot of past sins.

Merton shocked his friends when he turned away from the world in his mid-twenties in order to become a Trappist monk. He joined one of the strictest and most cloistered of all orders, the Cistercians of the Strict Observance (O.C.S.O.). The Trappists, as they are more commonly known, were once regarded to be the only "Green Berets" left in contemporary monasticism. The monks were required to get up in the middle of the night to pray, to sleep on boards of wood, to work in the fields more than study, and to wear woolen cowls even on the hottest of days. A simple set of hand signals replaced almost all talking in Trappist monasteries. Thomas Merton willingly exchanged a life full of choices for a highly disciplined one, and it made sense to me as described in his books.

I thought that I was truly free when I was almost twenty, loosening the knot of my childhood faith. Everything seemed up for grabs. But the notion of leaving Christianity behind was completely out of the question. I simply wanted to broaden my experience of God— not do something crazy.

Thomas Merton's early writings—especially *The Seven Storey Mountain*, an autobiography published when he was barely thirty years old, and *The Sign of Jonas*, a collection of journal entries written before and during the time that he wrote the autobiography— emphasize the power of the contemplative life and the courage, rather than the lack of it, that leads men into monasteries. I was intrigued.

The appeal of Thomas Merton for me was the difference between his life and mine, the contrast between his free spirit and my own constricted one, the model that he was for making life anew—finding God alone, down a path that seems so far from home. He lived and wrote beautifully and had a knack for eliminating all distance between himself and his readers. He also ran to the contemplative life for similar reasons that I desired it: annihilation in God. I liked the idea of what I thought it meant to become a monk: no one but God would ever expect anything of me again. It seemed as if an abbey would be a quiet place where I would have plenty of time to read and pray and be—to escape myself—far away from what I knew.

In the closing paragraphs to *The Seven Storey Mountain*, Merton said to God:

> You have called me here not to wear a label by which I can recognize myself and place myself in some kind of a category. You do not want me to be thinking about what I am, but about what You are. Or rather, You do not even want me to be thinking about anything much: for You would raise me above the level of that.

It's not that I wanted to convert to Catholicism; I wanted the same sort of anonymity of spirit and personality that a cloistered life in Kentucky might provide. A place where I could indulge my passions, all of which seemed to be about God.

During the summer that I turned nineteen, I visited Merton's Abbey of Gethsemani twice in six months after returning from Asia. On the first occasion, I drove from Chicago to Kentucky with Kristin, a good friend. As we made our way around Louisville and onto Highway 245 winding toward Bardstown, Kristin noticed not one, but two, dead cats along the side of the road. As I slowed to drive around them, we looked at each other without saying anything.

"What do your parents think of this interest of yours?" she asked, as we soon approached the driveway to the monastery.

"I haven't mentioned it to them," I said.

I didn't know what to make of my desires to become a monk, to remove myself from the world of fundamentalist Christian ambition to a life of praying in the woods. "The contemplative life is the most effective vocation," the retreat master at Gethsemani said to me one day. "The world needs us more than it needs more noise and chatter." I suspected that he was right, but I was alone in my thoughts and kept this idea from friends, family, and church.

I began reading the *Rule of St. Benedict*, the early medieval document that has guided the lives of Western monks for centuries. In fact, Benedict is named as one of the patron saints of Europe for the effect that his movement had in building and educating the continent. A love of study always came easily to me—a great inheritance from fundamentalism—and I was delighted by Benedict's injunctions to study. Chapter forty-eight of the Rule prescribes daily manual labor and holy reading for all monks. I also discovered in the pages of the Rule many other ideas that made good sense.

Chapter forty-nine explains that heartfelt prayer comes through grave humility and tears. I was taught that sort of seriousness early on. Other chapters instruct the monks to regard their abbot, those who are ill, and anyone who knocks on your door as Christ himself. This instruction, of course, comes from the Gospels (as does much of the Rule), but the practicality of how to follow such an injunction startled me. Chapter fifty-three explains that the same "awe of the rich" that people often feel is how we should regard the most lowly. I saw in monasticism a radical, counter-cultural response to the world as faithfulness to Christ, not unlike the radical faith I grew up with. Five of the chapters in the middle of the book (twenty-three to twenty-seven) are instructions on the who, when, and for what offenses one should be excommunicated, cast out from the community and from God's favor. I didn't like that at all, but it made sense to me. Fundamentalists never believed that trying hard always equals spiritual success. God might have other plans for your life.

A monk had never even crossed my path until I read Merton or spoke with the retreat director at Gethsemani. But when I explored what monks do, and how they measure a man's worth in the world, I felt that the life called me. Merton wrote:

Cistercian monks [make] five vows, at the time of [our] profession: poverty, chastity, obedience, stability, and conversion of manners. The whole meaning of the monastic vocation is summed up in these vows, which are given to the monk as a means of consecrating his life to God. They deliver him from the uncertainties and cares and illusions that beset the man of the world. They imply struggle and difficulty. They demand complete self-renunciation. They lead to a life perfectly hidden in Christ. They embrace the whole life of man and all his desires with a singular completeness.

Taking them one by one, I considered the monastic renunciations. Poverty would be easy, I thought; the pursuit of things was not high on my list of priorities, and besides, I was nineteen and couldn't imagine owning much. Chastity would be a blessing, I reasoned. I was exhausted by dating after only my teenage experience of it and, up until that time, I did not know the blessing of real love. Obedience and stability would be most difficult—having to do whatever a superior asked you to do without question. But I wanted guidance. I never really tended to rebellion, only questioning.

It is nearly impossible to consider such a life-changing idea without the help of others and yet I did. I did not ask many of my friends, and certainly not my family, for their opinions. In most cases, I thought I knew what I would hear.

Emily Dickinson wrote

> *The Soul unto itself*
> *Is an imperial friend—*
> *Or the most agonizing Spy*
> *An Enemy—could send*

and I felt just that.

I argued both sides in my head and finally decided that I couldn't make the leap to Catholicism. The thing that held me back was: What would my family and friends say? A Catholic monastery in Kentucky was almost as foreign to our experience as a Buddhist one in Japan.

There is a fascinating old book in my library called *Camping and Woodcraft* by Horace Kephart, published in two volumes in 1916–1917. Kephart lived in the Great Smoky Mountains and wrote about everything that one might need to know in order to survive in the wild of the American woods. In volume two, he has an intriguing chapter entitled "Bee Hunting."

Kephart describes how a backwoodsman can practice "lining" bees, when chancing upon them and if you are not entirely prepared for the more efficient means of regular bee hunting. This process "is to capture one of the insects and fasten to it, or stick into it, a small, downy feather, a bit of straw or thistle-down, or some other light thing by which he can distinguish the insect in its flight; then he liberates it, and follows it as far as he can by sight. The bee, bothered by its strange encumbrance, and finding that it cannot rid itself of the thing by its own exertions, goes home for help." This is great for the bee hunter, who follows the "marked bee," and perhaps a few others, until finding the hive. Like a marked bee, I was bothered by some foreign encumbrances, and finding that I couldn't completely rid myself of them, I went home.

Without too much hesitation, I put my feelings on hold and registered for a sophomore year at Wheaton

College in my hometown, the school made famous by Billy Graham. It was an educational "middle way" between the rejection of everyone I knew—had I transferred from Moody Bible Institute to, say, Reed College in Oregon, or the University of Wisconsin-Madison, two of my top choices—and the experiences of the previous year.

I quickly found the mentors that I was looking for to replace the ones I had left behind. Fundamentalism taught me the value and wisdom of older friends; I have always wanted the guidance of those who came before me, experienced teachers and mentors, and I have always listened to them.

Despite Wheaton College's conservative underpinnings, its classes and professors encouraged critical challenge to every assumption. In my first year, I became the research assistant to Arthur Holmes, chair of the philosophy department. We would meet twice each week to discuss the research I was doing on Christian Platonism in support of a book he was preparing to write. I loved the interchanges with him.

On another occasion, I was taking a seminar on the Protestant Reformation with one of the senior members of the history faculty. I chose as the subject for my paper, "The Doctrine of Justification by Faith from Augustine to Luther." The term "justification by faith" means, simply, that sinners are made right with God, or justified before God, by faith, as opposed to being justified by something else, such as doing good things.

Midway through the term, I remember going to my professor's office very urgently and asking, "Is it acceptable if I suggest in my paper that the apostle Paul got it wrong?"

"What do you mean?" he asked hesitantly.

"Well, in my research on what Augustine and Luther wrote about the doctrine of justification, I am realizing that so much of their arguments throw the issue back upon Paul, and what he wrote in his epistles. And, what Paul wrote in his epistles is really an interpretation of what Jesus taught in the Gospels, right? So, I'm wondering: May I suggest in my paper that Paul got it wrong?"

He told me it was okay to suggest that Paul got Jesus wrong. Although many issues of fundamentalist faith are set as immovable doctrine (and I was treading onto one of them with my questions), in other respects, the fundamentalist is the most thorough of Protestants, questioning everything. I learned from my fundamentalist education that we must own our faith, questioning things until we settle on what is ours. But for me, such questioning led to greater doubt, less truth. I was finding my way from religious certainty to reasonable doubt one step at a time.

Thomas Merton concludes *The Seven Storey Mountain* with a Latin sentence: *Sit finis libri, non finis quaerendi.* Despite Professor Kay's best intentions during our college summer tutorial, my Latin was mediocre at best, but this sentence roughly translates to: *Here ends the book, but not the searching.*

twelve

washing out my ears
belief I can live with

*Reef Knot—Known also as square or true knot.
Will not slip, unless used in tying a small cord or
rope to a thicker one. So long as the two ends are of
equal diameter this knot may be relied upon.*
—Horace Kephart

When a fundamentalist of any religion begins to slide
in what they can affirm as truth, there are always
borderlines that mark "in" from "out." Remarkably,
the lines are similar from tradition to tradition.

Do you believe that [your faith] is the one, true faith?

Do you believe that [your scriptures] are the unaltered,
unedited, direct revelation of God?

After these two questions, all of the rest become inconsequential. The majority of issues that preoccupy the majority of spiritual seekers are beside the point, to a fundamentalist. The fundamentalist wants to know whether or not you have accepted these two propositions as fact. In many ways, the line of demarcation between religious people today is the same as it always has been: there are those who can affirm the fundamentals with confidence, and there is everyone else.

Falling from that sort of certainty happens at differing velocities for different people, and a lot of the speed probably depends on whom you have around you. In my case, I remained connected to parents, family, childhood friends, all of which slowed me on my way down. But, it wasn't easy or comfortable.

One by one, it seemed, my friends were either frightened or appalled by my questions or by my answers to their questions. On one occasion, my greatest friend from high school would not accept that I might believe that people of other faiths might go to heaven. After a half hour of polite argument, she turned to look me dead in the eyes and said: "Is Jesus Christ the only way, the only truth, and the only life?"

"Not exactly," I said, as she flapped her arms into the air. "I don't think that that is what is meant by those words."

Then she asked me to leave her parent's home. We had spent hundreds of hours there over the last several years.

Seven years later, she was married and living in Atlanta. I found myself there, traveling for work, at exactly the same time as she was giving birth to twins.

Her mother had called my mother to share the good news. The next afternoon, I arranged to leave my conference early, and I drove over to the hospital during visiting hours in a rented car. I asked at reception for her room. The babies were there, a beautiful boy and a girl, as were her husband and her sister, with whom I had picnicked, played volleyball, and spent hundreds of hours. Within five minutes it was clear that I was not welcome, and I was asked to leave. She looked at me as if I had a poisonous snake wrapped around the crown of my head.

These slow separations of changing faith were agonizing. I would imagine that a slide toward separation and divorce, after years of loving marriage, would feel somewhat similar.

There was no question but that religious commitment would remain a part of my life. Fundamentalist faith had taught me, for instance, that there were no guts in agnosticism. Meditators, atheists, nihilists—these were all serious people, even if mistaken, but chronic fence-walkers had nothing to win or lose, and nothing to live for.

One Easter Sunday, my brother, Doug, was newly married and spending the day with his in-laws across town. I went to church with my parents and out to dinner afterward. Knowing that my beliefs were in flux and that I was questioning just about everything, my father wanted to test me.

"What are you planning to do after college, now, Jon?" he asked.

"I'm really not sure," I said. "Perhaps I'll do something unexpected."

"Like what, exactly?"

"I would like to have a simple job and live in a simple place. It doesn't matter what I do, only that I do it well," I explained.

My parents were puzzled. "What are you talking about? Do you mean, for instance, that you could become a plumber, a carpenter, an insurance salesman?"

"Sure," I said. "I could be really happy doing those sorts of things."

To their minds, it was as if I said I was thinking of moving to an island in the Caribbean to live on the beach and comb for lost valuables. We argued about what it meant to live a meaningful life, and it became clear that the only professional life worth pursuing was a religious one, like being a pastor or a missionary.

"I don't want to be big for God, in front of people, preaching, teaching, a superstar. I want a smaller life. Why can't I live small and still be a good Christian?"

"You can. Or, I mean, other people could," my mother replied earnestly, "but that is not enough for you. You can do really great things."

"But that is what I am saying," I argued. "It is possible to be great and not do what Dad does, or what Grandpa does, or what my uncles do. Right?" I'm not so sure, though, that I believed it when I said it.

Han Shan, the eighth-century Chinese poet, did all he could in order to do his religion right, but his efforts ultimately fell short. By middle age, he was left wanting to retire to the mountains and "wash out his ears." Han Shan wandered the mountains writing poems on cliffs, debunking the legalisms and certainties of faith. I sometimes feel the same today on our little mountain in Vermont.

I actually began to leave fundamentalist churches just when fundamentalist churches began to market themselves in savvy ways. The term fundamentalist, in fact, which was once a badge of honor for conservative, serious Christians, itself began to evolve. Fundamentalists in other world religions were giving Christian fundamentalists a bad name. So, we began to use the word "evangelical" to replace the f-word.

For a time, while I questioned just about everything, I joined one of the most popular evangelical groups in the country. Together with dozens of other students from Wheaton College, I began attending Willow Creek Community Church each Sunday morning, one of the new evangelical mega-churches, in the northern suburbs of Chicago. Each Sunday, we made the long drive from Wheaton to South Barrington, snaking our way through busy intersections and around strip malls.

The huge Willow Creek building didn't look at all like a church, by design. It could have been an exhibit hall for trade shows, or one of those enormous multiplexes. It was common to park almost half a mile away and still be in the asphalt Willow Creek parking lot; orange cones and attendants waving flags showed us to our spot in line.

The activity inside the church was designed to resemble traditional worship as little as possible. We attended more for the energy of the place than anything else. Plus, it was high entertainment. A live band on stage, dramatic fade-ins and fade-outs between acts, drama players and skits, and motivational talks that sounded very little like sermons. Bill Hybels—always referenced without the Rev.—started Willow Creek in a rented movie theater in Palatine, Illinois, in 1975 as an outreach to the unchurched, aiming to appeal to people through entertainment in a non-religious setting. At some point in the late 1980s, Willow Creek became the second largest church in America.

At the end of twelve months of experimenting with this new form of polished worship, I again began to crave asceticism. Exposed to the "best" of evangelical faith, I felt more and more alienated from God. The smooth performance of casual spirituality gave way in me to the desire for its opposite: silence and renewed obedience. I grew anxious to explore the possibility of a monastic vocation to its end this time, so I visited The Abbey of Gethsemani in Kentucky again in February of 1988 and made a reservation to return for a week of seeking God's discernment for my life during that coming December. I felt that God might want me to become a Trappist after all. It was again a means of expressing my desire to be completely devoted to faith, only a different sort of faith from what I really knew. Give me sweat and silence rather than slick and sophisticated, I thought.

It was not a coincidence that my plans for a retreat in December of 1988 coincided with the twentieth anniversary of Thomas Merton's death. While on a pilgrimage to the East that he had dreamed of and planned for a decade, Merton died while attending an interreligious conference of monastics in Bangkok. He was a klutz and accidentally electrocuted himself in the bathroom; not a heroic death, to be sure.

I prayed intently during those summer months, asking God for guidance, and I met with two of my Wheaton professors, asking veiled questions about Catholicism. Hesitantly, I brought up the subject with my parents at dinner one night.

"What in the world would you do as a monk!" my mother said, almost emotionally unable to be her usual, always-supportive self.

"Becoming a monk isn't about what you will do so much as it is about who you will be," I said, feeling good that I had absorbed enough monastic spirituality to be able to say such a thing almost on cue.

I was drawn to the monastic life because it seemed to stand for what I loved most about the faith of my fathers and mothers. I loved how counter-cultural it was. Monks were not supposed to seek power, or prestige, or money. They were disciples of Christ, following the will of God with a radical simplicity, hospitality, poverty, and faithfulness. But then, I also was drawn to the life of a monk because it seemed very different from my fundamentalism. I loved how miracles can happen in a monastery. The life was full of the Spirit and seemed to contrast with the cold beam of my rational faith. There are many things in life that show God's presence here and now, not just in history and Scripture, according to monastic spirituality. Sometimes the love of God can allow us to do things that do not make complete sense to those we love.

One serious obstacle to joining a monastic community for me, however, was that I have never found much comfort or satisfaction in religious groups. My non-denominational, independent brand of childhood faith taught me to feel more comfortable on my own than in congregations or fellowship groups. I have been gradually trying to unlearn those impulses over the decades since.

At about this time in my life, I became an Episcopalian, not as some of my friends did, through a special ceremony involving kneeling to kiss the bishop's ring. Rather, I simply attended my local parish with regularity, contributed money to its work and outreach, acted occasionally as lector or intercessor or reader during morning prayer; I volunteered to teach or sit in the pre-school during services; and I was generally involved in the community. But, I didn't formalize it. Even today, I am, by force of habit, what my tradition calls a "communicant." According to the *Book of Common Prayer*, a communicant is someone who will consistently "work, pray, and give for the spread of the kingdom of God." That's me.

Similarly, years later—but not many years ago—when I wrote and edited two books on Francis of

Assisi, many interviewers as well as acquaintances, knowing that I am neither a professor or a priest, asked: "Are you a member of the Third Order of Francis?"

The "Third Order" was established by St. Francis during his lifetime as a gathering of laypeople who wanted to follow his way of life and support the values that he espoused, while remaining in "the world." It was so-named after the "First Order" of Brothers Minor, now called Franciscans, and the "Second Order" of Sisters Clare had already been started.

Francis understood—after mothers scolded him for taking away their sons, and husbands worried aloud that their wives were listening to Clare too much—that not everyone should feel called to leave behind family relationships, work, and responsibilities. You can become a Franciscan at home where you are, Francis was explaining by creating the Third Order. Members of the Third Order have sometimes also been called Secular Franciscans. Today, there are international bodies of both Catholic and Anglican/Episcopal Third Order groups. I am not a member of any of them. To be honest, I usually reply to the question by saying: "When I reviewed the applications to join, the requirements for referrals, the years of proving postulancy before acceptance—I concluded that the spirit of Francis was not there." Francis of Assisi met his first brothers and sisters face-to-face and said what Jesus said, asking them to follow him and live his life. You were in.

I also must confess, I suppose, that I will never be a great fan of the organized and denominational church, of any stripe. I don't think, in fact, that we should ever be too settled in our denominational identities. At least on this point, my grandfathers would be proud of me (we were *independent* Baptists, not denominational Baptists).

Theologian H. Richard Niebuhr once wrote that it is easy for Christians to become too tied up with the culture. When we do, he said, "faith loses its force . . . discipline is relaxed, repentance grows formal, corruption enters with idolatry, and the church, tied to the culture which it sponsored, suffers corruption with it." I felt that monasticism might be the one option of Christian life where these conflicts could be avoided.

But I turned away from the monastic life. After many months of questioning, prayer, and simple waffling back and forth, I cancelled my reservation at the Abbey of Gethsemani. I had felt so compelled to join, desiring to love God and be loved by God completely, but I soon realized that God had a different plan for me. I began to understand that divine love comes in many forms, and in my case, it came in the person of my future wife and partner. We met, fell in love, and became engaged before that December 1988 appointment at the abbey ever came around on the calendar.

■ ■ ■ ■ ■ ■ ■ thirteen

he fumbles at your soul
following the love of God

And so it is with all things. If you are not happy,
act the happy man. Happiness will come later. So
also with faith. If you are in despair, act as though
you believed. Faith will come afterwards.
—Isaac Bashevis Singer

There are good reasons why in most of the world's religious traditions the heart and not the head is the center of the spiritual anatomy. The heart reverberates at times without our intention or our will, and symbolizes God inside of us, doing the same. Also, our heart feeds our spirit at times when our mind is not in step with either of them.

I did not intend to love Danelle. At twenty, I was preparing myself to enter the Trappist monastery and close the door on that sort of thing. But, it didn't happen that way. There are good reasons why abbeys require many years of a postulant before he may take vows to become a novice, and then more years before a novice may take vows to become a monk. My postulancy, of sorts, was lived outside of monastery walls, and I never made it very far.

Danelle and I met through her brother, David, who was for a time my best friend in college. David and I occasionally talked about his little sister, always in the context of what she was up to. She always seemed interested in things that were not of much interest to me, and she dated guys that I knew.

Our first date came as a result of one of those silly, childish bargains that kids make with each other in order to avoid the appearances of a date. I cannot remember now exactly what it was, but I think we made a bet that involved me buying her dinner if she won. She did, and we went out.

Getting a date like that was a very short evolution from how dates got started in elementary school. I have been puzzled, over the last few years, as to why my kids have not seemed to take part in the dating rituals that I understood in fifth and sixth grade. If you had a special liking for someone, you wouldn't tell her directly; you would tell her friend. You wouldn't say: "Now, don't tell anyone," because you wanted her to tell. That was the whole point. Another way to communicate your infatuation would be to write a note. We were big on writing notes. I believe that my mother received three different admonishments from my teachers in grammar school when I was caught writing notes, or passing notes, in class. One of my notes, in fact, was read aloud to the class by my sixth grade teacher, Mrs. Bartlett.

Dear Kim,
Do you like me?
 Yes
 No
I think I like you.
Jon

We would fold the note in quarters and hand it stealth-ily to its recipient—occasionally via an intermediary, but only if he was of the utmost trustworthiness. Well, one morning—the day that I wanted to ascertain Kim's affections—Stan was less than trustworthy. He handed my note to Mrs. Bartlett, thinking it would be a funny joke to play on me.

I could have tried such a tactic with Danelle in college, but I wouldn't have enjoyed the answer. After that first date, we really hated each other. She thought that I was full of myself, cold, and uncaring, and I thought that she was foolish, flip, and didn't take herself seriously enough. We were probably both right. Each of us told David that we had no interest in the other, and it was all true.

The poet Emily Dickinson somehow understood love—both divine and human—even though she had remarkably few experiences in relationships. She lived almost hermit-like in the Amherst, Massachusetts, home of her parents throughout her adult life after having spent one year at a nearby college. From childhood to her death at age fifty-six, Emily made only a handful of sojourns away from Amherst and never farther than Washington, D.C. She knew romantic love, and she knew the tight love of God that came through her strict, Calvinist upbringing, as well as a close friendship that bordered on the romantic with the married clergyman Charles Wadsworth of Philadelphia.

Emily's solitude somehow taught her many things that most of us go through life missing out on completely. She learned to argue with God, and to seek God in the shadows of her emotions and doubts, as well as her convictions. She knew that it is almost impossible to understand human love without being a part of divine love; they are inseparably intertwined. She wrote wise lines about human love that are neither sentimental nor sad, and she wrote these reflections about divine love that are neither pious nor settled:

He fumbles at your Soul
As Players at the Keys
Before they drop full Music on—
He stuns you by degrees—
Prepares your brittle Nature
For the Ethereal Blow—
By fainter Hammers—further heard—
Then nearer—Then so slow

Your Breath has time to straighten—
Your Brain—to bubble Cool—
Deals——One—imperial—Thunderbolt—
That scalps your naked Soul

I yearned for divine love, and was not able to discover it fully until I experienced real human love.

My grandmother used to say to me: "God loves you and so do *I!*" She would put the emphasis on that last word and hug me tightly around the belly, her four feet and something frame tiny next to mine from about my thirteenth year on. She would really squeeze, I remember, and I can still feel her head tight in my sternum, when I was a teenager, as if she wanted to push that love right up inside me.

Perhaps divine love is like that; it can feel taken away from us when human love is absent from our lives, and it can also pierce our defenses the way human love can. My grandmother gave me the love of God by force. I didn't have a choice but to take it in. To have rejected it would have been to reject her, and I wasn't about to do that.

Following Emily Dickinson's remarkable phrases for love: Neither my breath nor Danelle's breath, my brain nor Danelle's brain, needed straightening or cooling after our first several encounters. I actually had little room in my psyche for romantic love or any of the feelings that would cause buckling knees or sweaty brows of nervousness on a date. I cannot say, either, that I was caught up in romance with God. I was caught up in trying to figure out God. Love, I soon realized, was something different. Love of both kinds—divine and human—came later.

I was especially wary of dating after high school because I knew what it meant. "Any date is a potential wife," I was taught in church, "and so, you had better only date a girl that could be your mate for life, your future partner." We were supposed to measure any desired date against a ledger of what was necessary in a Christian wife. Up until that point in my life, my list boiled down to the simple reality that any girl I dated needed to want the life of pastor's spouse, and needed to seem ideally suited for it. Well, that cut down my options tremendously. Danelle, for instance, wasn't about to play the church organ, stand in a greeting line after services, or rally the women's auxiliary group. Those were the traditional ways of a pastor's spouse.

Like most college students, I didn't know exactly what I wanted. I was searching for love—from God, family, friends, maybe a lifetime partner—and it all seemed wrapped up as the same thing. "He fumbles at your Soul. He stuns you by degrees." Dickinson was writing about the mixed-up confusion of divine and human love.

I also had to figure out what I might do with my life. If I couldn't find my way through Bible college and to that leadership role in fundamentalist Christianity, and if turning around and becoming a Catholic monk was not right, either, I reasoned that perhaps the next best thing would be to become a pastor in one of the "mainline" denominations. I wasn't sure what brand of Christian I now was, but I knew that I needed to figure that out.

For as long as I can remember, I have wanted to grow up and grow older. The "next thing" was always more appealing than the current thing. While in junior high, I wanted desperately to be in high school; while in high school, I wanted desperately to leave home and go to college; and in college, I wanted to get on to something more meaningful.

I first heard the phrase "parish priest" from the father of one of my friends in college. He was a Presbyterian pastor in Kentucky, and we were sitting in his living room. Wood-paneled walls were lined with gorgeous bookcases filled with books by authors that I was interested in. I asked him where he went to seminary. "Princeton," he said. I asked him how he decided to become a pastor. He replied: "Ever since college, all I wanted to be was a parish priest. It is a great life; you should consider it, too." The phrase confused me. A parish *priest*. How could I ever be a *priest*? When I was a child, priests were only found in the branches of faith that our church considered wrong, or misguided. My friend's father might as well have said that I should become a swami, or an imam.

But, I tried the word on. I began using it and it began to make sense. This is often how it worked for me as a young adult: words took on meanings gradually as I used them in my life—another gift of my fundamentalism.

Not only do words matter, but using them leads to understanding them.

Soon, studying to become a priest became my stated goal, my way of fulfilling God's will for my life. Even now, as I say the word out loud, my ears still shock at the sound of it. We do not easily unlearn our prejudices. Sometimes the least we can do is remain aware of them.

So, during my junior year of college, when it became clear that I was far enough along to graduate at least a semester early, I instead enrolled in seminary in Chicago. One of my college professors recommended the school, as he was about to begin teaching there: North Park Theological Seminary, on Chicago's north-west side. It was rooted in the Swedish Pietist tradition, attached to the Evangelical Covenant Church of America, and noted for its wide acceptance of belief and practice. North Park was good advice, and a good choice for me.

I arranged my college class schedule so that I had two free days each week to drive downtown and attend classes at the seminary. The commute was nearly an hour and a half each way, but I didn't mind. I did that all during my senior year and then took on a more traditional course load at North Park after college graduation.

I loved the study at seminary. What could be better than reading, discussing, and studying all matters related to Christian faith and thought? I waited on tables at night and studied all day, often sitting for hours on end in the stacks of the school library. I became a student

assistant to two of the professors so that I could build
those sorts of mentor relationships that I so enjoyed.
All in all, it was a great time in my life, but it also didn't
take long for me to realize that I was not the typical
seminary student.

At most seminaries, the primary student demographic
is second-career people, usually in their mid-thirties,
married, often with kids at home. My classmates were
insurance salespeople, actors, acting clergy needing
proper credentials, social workers, retail store man-
agers, and energetic Christians who wanted to follow
what they felt was God's will for their lives by pulling
up roots and training to be clergy.

Most of my classmates lived in low-rent apartments,
having left behind good jobs and careers, and they
wanted to make what was a transitional time for their
families as quick and painless as possible. They were in
class in order to reach a clear goal—to get a church. I
was only twenty-one years old and without many
expectations. I had recently left all certainty of what
was supposed to happen in my life behind. I didn't
know what I was supposed to do, exactly. I thought
that we were in something like graduate school, there
to learn, discuss, read, and study.

Meanwhile, Danelle and I began dating and taking a
liking to each other. We began scheduling classes
together, spending time together in the evenings, and
falling quickly in love. We each had those faults that
we sensed in the other at first, but we improved each
other. We dated from early spring into early summer

and before the end of our junior year, only a few months after we started seriously dating, we were engaged.

I felt my life changing both from within and from without. My yearning for God was in my love for Danelle, and God's love for me was delivered beautifully and effectively in Danelle's love for me. The following summer after college graduation we were married at Danelle's home church in Richmond, Virginia.

I might wish a fundamentalist childhood for my own two kids for no other reason than that they might know what it is like to save the intimacies of marriage for marriage itself. It is easy to poke fun at fundamentalist sexual ethics, but I don't. I am grateful for what I did not know until Danelle and I were joined together.

Fundamentalists do crazy, unfortunate things such as posting the Ten Commandments in public places and rejecting the distribution of condoms to fight AIDS and other sexually transmitted diseases. But the ideal of union with a single partner (sustained perhaps only in fundamentalism today), and the ideal of becoming one in marriage, are still the most beautiful possibilities of human love. These ideals show how human love mirrors the intimacy of the union with God; other loves do not just fade into the background—they wither away, leaving room for only one. At the time in my life when Danelle and I married, I was undergoing a slow transformation from faithfulness to Christ alone—in my longing for a marriage like that between a monk and Christ—and the love that was opening inside of me for

Danelle. These loves are not all that different. As the Song of Songs says, "My beloved is mine, and I am his."

I am sure that Danelle would not be flattered by much of the language in the ancient Song of Songs— her hair is not like a flock of goats, her teeth not a flock of sheep, and her neck is not exactly the tower of David—but the ideal was still ours. "Thou hast ravished my heart, my sister, *my* spouse; thou hast ravished my heart with one of thine eyes, with one chain of thy neck. How fair is thy love, my sister, my spouse! How much better is thy love than wine!"

We honeymooned briefly in England, visiting churches and cathedrals and Covent Garden, and driving ourselves to Hay-on-Wye, a medieval book town on the border with Wales. But when we returned to our lives in Chicago, the gazelles were no longer leaping as high as they were in the days after our wedding. Danelle took an office job that offered benefits and a meager salary, so that I could continue going to seminary. She worked days and I worked nights, after classes. We were usually exhausted, even on the weekends.

I enjoyed my professors in seminary enormously. Stephen Graham, Philip Anderson, Paul Holmer, Donald Dayton, Burton Nelson, Robert Johnston, Priscilla Pope-Levison, David Scholer, they were all terrific. But, I was a kid. I knew that I didn't have the character or the experience to be a pastor or priest to anyone. Why would my family, my home church, or the dean of the seminary assume that I could? I began to relate to that old Groucho Marx/Woody Allen joke: "I wouldn't want to be a part of any club that would have someone like me for a member."

I remember asking for a meeting with the dean of the seminary one morning, after two and a half years of seminary study. I needed counsel and considered him a friend. The previous year I had taken his course on Religion in Contemporary Literature, had written a paper on John Updike's novel *The Unicorn*, that he praised, and had spent an evening at his house for dinner. We knew each other, and so I felt comfortable speaking frankly with him.

The dean's office was dimly lit, in a corner of the campus where one-hundred-year-old maple trees lay shade around the windows. He pointed me to a wing-back leather chair in the corner of the room as he was finishing something at his desk. I sat, and without looking up, he said: "So, Jon, what's up?"

"I have a problem that I think makes it necessary for me to leave seminary," I said. That got his attention. He looked up and stepped over to the other wingback chair.

"What is it?"

"I don't think that I like people enough," I replied.

He was obviously taken aback, but tried to look as ordinary as possible.

"What does that mean, exactly?"

"I see others in class and on assignment, happy to be here, happy to be on their way to getting a church to lead, a flock to shepherd—all of that—and all I feel is resentment. Even the meaningless banter of greetings

in the morning drives me nuts: 'How are you?' 'Fine.'
'And you?' 'Good.' I can't do that sort of thing. I guess
that I don't like people enough; I can't be a leader of
anyone."

My dean was unprepared for this sort of conversation.
Needing to be off to teach a class, he muttered a few
reassurances and then we were done. I finished up the
semester's classes and then quit. Again my postulancy
was a failure.

As school ended I felt nothing but dread. Suddenly
and seriously, I was without real career options. For
twenty-two years, all that I knew was that I was going to
be a pastor, then an Episcopalian priest, leading people
to find God, speaking with authority from behind a pulpit. First, I had walked away from the fundamentalist
faith that defined me, and then I was about to leave the
seminary that accepted me early, taught me a great
deal, and finally—the bitter reality—was that I had lost
my last clear path to a job. Seminary was a career track;
there was a church at the end of it. College led to
seminary and seminary led to preaching or teaching or
some other sort of full-time religious work. Then, a few
months later, Danelle and I decided to move away from
Chicago, cross-country to Boston, and so we very truly
set ourselves adrift in search of a new start.

knocking everywhere

coming to terms with dogma

At least—to pray—is left—is left—
Oh Jesus—in the Air—
I know not which thy Chamber is—
I'm knocking—everywhere
—Emily Dickinson

I imagine that all people of faith—if they really want to own theirs—have to argue with the faith of their parents. I did. Fundamentalist faith was full of dogma, and in order for me to reconcile with both faith and family after wandering away from the certainty and conservative leanings of those teachings, I had to figure out where I stood with regard to their underpinnings.

I didn't really understand how slowly this process of internal debate was in my life, until Danelle and I had children of our own. Kids with questions led me to finally answer some of those same questions for myself. For that reason, let me jump ahead in the chronology of this narrative in order to explain how I wrestled with dogma, re-imagined it, and found peace with my faith.

I am sure that I'm not the only parent who has had difficulty talking with his children about religion precisely because his kids raise objections to some of the same things that I've spent a lifetime doubting—or, at least, struggling to accept.

When my daughter was old enough to read, she began doubting that what she read was really true. Imagine the shock that super-parent feels when his six-year-old says to him after church: "That stuff isn't really *true!*" I thought for sure that I was doing something wrong.

Given my own childhood immersion in fundamentalism, and my slow ebbing away from it as an adult, Danelle and I did not have our children baptized as infants. I in particular wanted them to, in the words of my childhood faith, "make an informed decision" for themselves. So, we waited until after they were each at least six years old to have them baptized, even though this is not how it is supposed to be done in the Episcopal Church. (Episcopalians will usually baptize you as an infant and then in the pre-teen years you may choose the "lesser" sacrament of confirmation to affirm the promises of your baptism.) Another problem with waiting was that neither of our kids at that point wanted to do it. I ran to it when I was their age, but I also had the active threat of hell on my heels.

At just the time when we wanted our daughter and our son to be baptized, she, at least, was already aware enough to know that a lot of what is said in church does not make obvious sense. For instance, she had heard time and again the prayer that is part of the confession of sins recited each Sunday morning:

> Almighty God, Father of our Lord Jesus Christ, maker of all things, judge of all men: We acknowledge and bewail our manifold sins and wickedness, which we from time to time most grievously have committed, by thought, word, and deed, against thy divine Majesty, provoking most justly thy wrath and indignation against us. We do earnestly repent, and are heartily sorry for these our misdoings; the remembrance of them is grievous unto us, the burden of them is intolerable. Have mercy upon us. . . .

"Oh, yeah, like we should feel *sooo* sorry!" she used to exclaim to me, just after the service ended and just beyond the earshot of others.

"We should be sorry for the things that we do that are wrong, don't you think?" I would try.

"I don't think that I do anything that wrong," she would explain. "And it's not like God is 'oh-so-great' and in such *ma*-jes-ty, while we are little nothings!"

I was stunned by the vehemence of her reactions to simple prayers. I didn't think that anyone was paying that close attention to the words we were repeating.

After her baptism, it was the Communion rail that became the most interesting place for encountering her objections. I didn't really understand for myself very clearly why we were "eating his flesh" and "drinking his blood"—it has been a lifelong struggle for me—and I am sure that I didn't explain my thoughts very clearly to my kids when they were young.

I had come to believe that it was God's love that motivated the incarnation of Christ, and that love was the primary reason for which Christ died on the cross. But that isn't the fundamentalist interpretation of the events. Fundamentalists, and many other Christians as well, point to a doctrine called "the atonement" to explain that Christ had to become incarnate, suffer, and die in order to *atone* for our sins. The idea is this: Adam and Eve committed the first sin against God in the Garden of Eden. That sin has been transmitted from mother to child for millennia and, as a result, each person is guilty of what we called "original sin" from the moment that they emerge from the womb. Original sin means a nature or predisposition to sin that is already in us.

The doctrines of original sin and of the atonement were at the heart of what I had been questioning since my earliest days in seminary. The fundamentalist theory explained that none of the restrictions or proscriptions of the Old Testament could do anything to ultimately "save" humankind from sin. The sacrifices of animals and the commandments were asked for by God, but never added up to salvation. In the Sermon on the

Mount, Jesus said: "Think not that I am come to destroy the law, or the prophets: I am not come to destroy, but to fulfill." We believed his intended meaning to be that the fulfillment of the law could only come through the Messiah, Christ, and his breaking of the bond (a bond that would otherwise carry us to hell) of original sin through the atonement. God had to become human in Christ in order to take on the sins of the world and pay for them with the blood sacrifice of his very life. All that remains for us today, we believed, is to accept that this is what happened. "For I say unto you, that except your righteousness shall exceed the righteousness of the scribes and Pharisees [who followed the old law], ye shall in no case enter into the kingdom of heaven."

I didn't want to explain faith to my children in terms of Christ dying to satisfy a debt for us; of God having a masochistic will that Jesus be flogged, dragged through the streets, and nailed to a tree like a criminal; God is not in the business of demanding human agony as a prerequisite for obtaining freedom.

It was precisely this dogma of fundamentalist faith that I wanted desperately to avoid in talking with my kids. So, then, how to explain it all? Danelle and I didn't do it very well at the time, and so Sarah treated Communion flippantly.

On the first occasion of trouble, Sarah received the host in the palm of her hand and took a nibble. She turned to me at the Communion rail and said in full voice, "Ughh! Tastes terrible!"

On the second occasion, as I approached the rail and knelt in my place beside the woman kneeling next to me, Sarah remained standing behind. She wasn't about to approach and kneel. I turned around and gave her an urging look. Nothing. So I reached back and pulled her toward me, and then she plopped reluctantly into place.

Since my early adult questioning of dogma first began, my experience of Communion has been so personal that I don't know how to explain its importance to my children. I want to hunger for God at the Communion rail. I make most sense of what I am doing there through the postures of accepting the bread and the wine. Psalm 84 speaks to this inner desire: "How amiable *are* thy tabernacles, O LORD of hosts! My soul longeth, yea, even fainteth for the courts of the LORD: my heart and my flesh crieth out for the living God. O LORD God of hosts, hear my prayer: give ear, O God of Jacob. For a day in thy courts *is* better than a thousand. I had rather be a doorkeeper in the house of my God, than to dwell in the tents of wickedness." I want to kneel before God; I want to accept the host in the palm of my hand; I want to drink from the cup without regard for twenty-first century fears of catching the cold of the person kneeling next to me.

I have come to believe that Jesus died because of what he preached; he died showing us how to have a relationship with God. I meet Jesus at the Communion rail, and I want to hunger and thirst for righteousness, leaving most of the explaining to the mystery of faith that we proclaim in the Episcopal Church: "Christ has died. Christ has risen. Christ is coming again." But that's me. My daughter cannot see the value in mystery, although I want both of my children to experience it firsthand.

If fundamentalism taught me to protest, I guess that I unwittingly passed this on to my daughter. In my church while growing up, we revered the Hebrew prophets, as they railed against the religious leaders of their day. We looked to the heroes of the Protestant Reformation—Martin Luther and the early Anabaptists—who stood up to the established church and pointed out what was wrong. Wherever Jeremiah's, or Luther's, or my father's certitude and presumption came from, perhaps mine did also. I have never doubted my right to question matters of faith that seem to need questioning. I also like it that my daughter has a respect for protest, a sense of questioning, earnestness for faith, and the belief that words should not be spoken without meaning.

But questioning something as central as the fundamentalist doctrine of the atonement—that makes me nervous, even today. If Jesus came primarily to love us and show us the way to the Father, then the traditional doctrine of hell is also called into question. I certainly questioned it in my wrestling with dogma after seminary, and I still do.

"You flatter yourself into thinking that there is no hell, or that it does not apply to you," one of my friends once said. But while I may no longer believe in a literal place of hell with my head, my heart still fears it. I cannot be glib about it. There may not be fundamentalist clergy in Christianity declaring fatwas against those who deny the basics of faith, but they often teach that people like me will be going to hell when they die.

I have wondered many times if I could or should renounce every ounce of questioning thought and turn back to fundamentalism. I would be received like a convert from Judaism or Islam to Christianity, one who saw the errors of his ways. I could probably become a star on the prophecy preaching tours. My testimony would inspire all who listened. I can imagine exactly how that would feel, and I like that feeling.

I heard many vivid sermons on hell as a child, and many of them referred to the most famous hell-fire sermon of them all: Jonathan Edwards' "Sinners in the Hands of an Angry God." He preached it on July 8, 1741, as a guest lecturer in Enfield, Connecticut, but it has been preached, in different forms, by fundamentalists ever since.

The anthropomorphic use of God's hands, active in torturing those who disbelieve, or live unholy lives, made perfect sense to me as a child.

The God that holds you over the pit of hell, much as one holds a spider; or some loathsome insect, over the fire, abhors you, and is dreadfully provoked: his wrath towards you burns like fire; he looks upon you as worthy of nothing else, but to be cast into the fire; he is of purer eyes than to bear to have you in his sight; you are ten thousand times more abominable in his eyes, than the most hateful venomous serpent is in ours. You have offended him infinitely more than ever a stubborn rebel did his prince; and yet, it is nothing but his hand that holds you from falling into the fire every moment. It is to be ascribed to nothing else, that you did not go to hell last night; that you were suffered to awake again in this world, after you closed your eyes to sleep. And there is no other reason to be given, why you have not dropped into hell since you arose in the morning, but that God's hand has held you up.

You might want to think that Edwards was speaking about people on the outside—people not present in the pews to listen to his ranting—but he wasn't. He was speaking relentlessly about sinners in the hands of an angry God, and those sinners were the people sitting before him, the people in church.

There is no other reason to be given why you have not gone to hell, since you have sat here in the house of God, provoking his pure eyes by your sinful, wicked manner of attending his solemn worship. Yea, there is nothing else that is to be given as a reason why you do not this very moment drop down into hell.

But there are other ways to look at how God works in our lives. Grace is always reaching out toward us. It is not so much a lightning bolt as it is a steady rain, or

at times, shower after shower after shower—and this is
what I would like my children to know. This is what
I came to know in the years after I left seminary, as I
struggled to come to terms with what I believed,
without some of those original "fundamentals."

■ ■ ■ ■ ■ ■ ■ fifteen

a wild night
and a new road

death is full of new birth

All living beings love one another (and eat one another) and they are all joined in the vast process of birth, growth, reproduction and death.
—Ernesto Cardenal, *Love*

When Danelle and I packed up the stuff from our grungy basement apartment in West Chicago in late October of 1991—after I dropped out of seminary—and we moved to Boston, our future was full of opportunities. Questions and doubts about dogma and other things would come soon, but we were optimistic. A change of scenery was needed.

Danelle drove the rental truck most of the way while I drove our old Nissan with three cats in carriers in the back seat and a litter box on the floor.

We left Chicago behind just twenty-four hours after our final day at work. We had no jobs to go to in Boston, only job interviews for me. Still, we were optimistic about taking this leap into the unknown. We said to ourselves: *We are young. When else will we feel free enough to do this sort of thing?*

Danelle's elderly cousin, who was just entering an assisted-living facility, owned an enormous old house in Lynn, Massachusetts, on the North Shore. It was one of those houses that you drive by today and wonder how much it must cost to heat in January. It stood three stories high and at one time must have been a lovely place to live.

Mary Baker Eddy was born in Lynn, and it used to be the successful shoe manufacturing center of New England, but no longer. We soon learned that the city had a terrible reputation. The high school dropout rate was the highest of any city north of Boston, and kids were selling crack on the street corners. Working-class families were losing their jobs and trying to move away. In fact, the day after we moved to town, we counted twelve houses for sale on the two miles of road with its linked stoplights leading to our house near the shore, and the number increased to twenty-two in the next six months. We were in the middle of a recession, but Danelle and I were oblivious to it.

We were excited about the move because it was an adventure of uncertainty, and it held the promise of living by the ocean. After spending many a summer on Cape Hatteras, North Carolina, with her family, Danelle thought of a home three blocks from the shore as an idyllic place of cool breezes and salt air.

We arrived on the Massachusetts Turnpike at about 10 p.m. on the evening of November 2, 1991, and as we approached the city of Boston, we saw signs of flooding and downed trees and debris everywhere. When we went through downtown—because we were not clever enough to avoid it—we saw power lines shimmering on wet pavement and crews working under temporary lighting hanging from the tops of trucks. While we wound our way somehow through the old Boston streets toward Route 1A, it seemed clear that quite a storm had come through the day before. As it turned out, we had moved to town the day after "the perfect storm," later made famous by a best-selling book and popular movie by that name. It was an auspicious introduction to New England.

That evening, we moved our belongings into the old house in Lynn. The place had been unoccupied and was dirty. We slept on the floor that night, not wanting to bother with hauling our bed out of the truck and putting it together late at night. The next morning, though, the sun shone brightly. Leaving the full truck sitting in the driveway, we walked the short distance to the beach, overlooking Nahant Island and, beyond it, to the Atlantic.

We had to pinch our noses because the stench was so bad. The Lynn beach is plagued by seaweed bacteria that smells awful as it rots in the sun. Years earlier, the town of Lynn disrupted the ecosystem of the bay and beach by constructing a causeway to the nearby island of Nahant. Ever since that time, the seaweed has tended to get stuck near shore in Lynn to rot, and stink. There have been efforts to fix the problem over the years, but none has ever quite worked.

There were other problems in our first days in Massachusetts, as well. A job interview that I had pre-arranged from Chicago turned into a second interview, and then a third, with the owner of the company. It was a Christian company with a fundamentalist mission statement, and he asked me about my personal beliefs. I answered honestly that things were changing for me, and I no longer saw myself within that world. I explained that I understood very well where I had come from and that I was respectful of it, but it wasn't me anymore. It was a job that I was overqualified for, but I didn't get it.

After a month of these disappointments, I went to work at a theological bookstore in Central Square, Cambridge, and Danelle at a flower shop in Lexington. We drove together each morning to Lexington and parked at the flower shop; I took a bus and a train from there to Cambridge. I still miss the bus and the time it gave me to read.

That winter was terribly cold in the dilapidated old house on Nahant Lane, Lynn. We couldn't afford to travel to see family at Christmastime, and so my parents came to see us. They did not hide their distaste for the neighborhood, the house, or our job prospects. "How can you live in this drafty old house?" they asked. And: "Are you really happy?" We were. We found our circumstances surprisingly romantic. But their visit was strained at best.

Our greatest joy was the discovery of another Episcopal Church, this one in Marblehead, Massachusetts, that seemed to speak to our need for beauty in liturgy, music, and prayer. We settled into the warmth of a local community of faith.

But several weeks later, as winter began slowing down, Danelle began not feeling well. She had a headache every day for a week, but continued to go to work each morning. We needed the money. The headaches became worse the following week; they were not going away, even with frequent doses of aspirin. Her whole body began to feel worn down. On a Friday morning, she wasn't well enough to go to work, and so we visited the doctor. It didn't take the doctor more than a few minutes to see that fluid was building in Danelle's belly, and he sent us downtown to have tests run at the Tufts-New England Medical Center. Within two hours, she was admitted to the Infectious Diseases unit.

My first instinct was to turn to faith in the midst of crisis—an essential, valuable piece of my fundamentalist inheritance. I was in church alone that Sunday, while Danelle slept in a hospital bed in Boston, and I prayed for healing. I cried all during the Eucharist.

A week later when Danelle was still in the hospital, and there was not yet a diagnosis, my mother-in-law drove up from Virginia to stay with me. We then made the drive to the hospital together each day in order to sit with Danelle during her many tests.

We met many physicians during the month that Danelle spent in the hospital. Tufts-NEMC is a training hospital for post-graduate residents, and every day one or two of them would come into Danelle's room and ask the same, basic questions: "When did the fever begin?" "Do you feel any pain or discomfort in your arms or legs?" "Does your family have a history of any chronic illness?" They would write her answers down quickly on their clipboards, studiously examining her body. To this day, we wonder if Danelle's case is the subject of footnotes in the dissertations of Boston medicine.

Three of the editors of the *New England Journal of Medicine* came to her bedside to examine her, ask questions, and consult with the attending physician. She was tested for AIDS, Multiple Sclerosis, any number of tropical diseases, even *Angiostrongylus cantonensis*, a parasite of rats rarely passed to humans, but with the clean-up we had done in the Lynn basement, we wondered. An expert in parasitology was called in from out-of-state, but uncovered nothing that led to a diagnosis.

Faith suffers anger and confusion. I remember the rage that I eventually felt toward our rector when he failed to visit Danelle in the hospital, week after week. Each Sunday, as I enjoyed the worship that I had grown to love, during the homily I would ruminate on his thoughtlessness for Danelle. Afterwards, on my way out,

I would remind him that Danelle was still at New England Medical, and he would say, "Yes, I must get down there one of these days."

Eventually, after almost five weeks, Danelle's fever subsided and the fluid in her belly began to go away. The color only returned to her cheeks after two more weeks of recuperating at home. Our primary physician at the hospital concluded that her case would simply be known as a "fever of unknown origin," and he wondered if it had been caused by something as yet unknown to science. Perhaps she picked up something while handling those bundles of glorious flowers that had come from South America.

I can only imagine what trauma it must be to bury a spouse, especially after so short a period together as Danelle and I had had up until that time. For years after her illness, and up until this writing, I was never willing to discuss what had happened. If you asked me about it, I would have given back only short, one-sentence answers. I made it clear that I wanted to talk about something else. Those godly eyes that I learned were watching me as a child were looking too intently at me during those days when Danelle was in the hospital. I was glad to keep them at bay. I didn't want the intimacy that God seemed to want from me. I couldn't even pray, "Don't make me like Job. Please don't take away my only family," because I feared too much that saying it might cause it to happen. I knew, from my childhood faith, that God listens, and I didn't want to give God any ideas about how to make me rely more exclusively on him.

But in Danelle's serious illness, and our fears about death, we found another new life. We came together as a couple, at that time, in ways that remind me again of the Song of Songs. We saw our union and our partnership being as full of divine love as it was of human love. I no longer fear death; in so many ways it is the fullness of life. Emily Dickinson once said, "Dying is a wild night and a new road." Our first year in Boston was certainly that, and death had set us on a new road.

A few years later, after Danelle's full recovery, we were on vacation in Italy with my family: my mom and dad, my brother and sister-in-law, and Danelle and me. Somewhere between Portofino and Parma we stopped for the night and found one of those ubiquitous, charming side-street cafes for dinner.

My mother was no closer to death than the rest of us at that time, but as she was about to turn sixty, she thought about it a lot more often. So, as I sprinkled romano on my spaghetti alla vongole, she said, "I would like you to cremate me when I'm gone."

"Really?" Danelle, replied. I think Danelle was the only other person not chewing.

"Yes, I think so," Mom said. "Dad and I have discussed it and we think cremation is best."

Now, since my brother and I were very young, mom has always wanted to discuss serious issues. We were never a family for much frivolous talk. For instance, long before it was fashionable, Mom said to my brother and me (we were probably eight and ten): "Do you guys want to talk about sex?"

"Uhhh, not really."

"It's okay, we should talk about it," she said. And, so we did. Again and again, or, so it seemed. Mom insisted on talking things through.

So, it was no great surprise when she started a conversation about how we should dispose of her body when she stops breathing. It was typical dinner conversation.

"What do *you* think?" she said, looking at me.

"I don't like it," I said.

"Really? What about you?" she said, turning to my older brother.

"I don't agree with cremation," he said.

"Well, well. Isn't that interesting," Mom replied, shooting a quick glance at my father sitting next to her.

My brother had become a professor of church history at a Midwestern seminary, and it often seemed that he knew just about everything there is to know about the history of Christian thought. As it turned out, his objections to the idea of cremating my mother were based on an analysis of the opinions of the early church fathers and Christian tradition. He mentioned a few examples of what our theological forefathers thought of the idea. His arguments made good sense.

My opinions were much less rational. I was in the midst of my questioning and doubting after leaving seminary. "I just don't like it," I began. "It would seem wrong to incinerate your body when you die."

Mom said, "But, *I* will be gone. You know that, of course. What was me will be departed."

"Yes and no," I said, still unsure of what I was saying. "Even if you accept that the body and the soul are completely distinct, and when the body stops functioning the soul lives on somewhere else—it is still wrong to obliterate the body of a person. Yours are the cheeks I have kissed, the hands I have held. There is a connection of some kind between our love and our bodies. Isn't that also the reason why organ donation is so precious, not just because someone else might be able to see with your eyes, but because your eyes are a remarkable gift to give, even after you have stopped using them?"

Mom was surprised that we would object. As it turned out, my parents had been discussing this issue with many of their long-time friends—spiritual/political conservatives, all of them—and they had all come to this decision together. One of their older friends, in fact, had recently passed away after a long illness and had delighted (literally) in planning his own cremation.

My parents' parents, who were young adults during the Great Depression, would never have considered cremation as an option. Much like my brother's opinion, my grandparents would have objected to cremation on traditional grounds. You just didn't do it if you were a Christian in America. Cremation was something done by atheists and Hindus, they thought.

Times have changed. My own conservative parents don't want anyone visiting their gravesites. And they desperately don't want open-casket funerals.

"Dust to dust, that is what seems right," Mom said at dinner.

My parents are of a generation that has already watched its parents die. They didn't like the nursing home dirtiness of it, and they quietly vowed to try and take care so that—when their own time came—not only would they not bother their children as slow-dying financial burdens, but they would clean up the mess they left. A tidy urn.

Our passing conversation stuck to me, and I later realized that Danelle's serious illness had changed forever how I felt about bodies, and death, and resurrection. When we returned from the trip to Italy, I composed a letter to my parents. I reproduce it here because, in many ways, it culminates my faith journey from fundamentalist childhood to the beliefs and faith that I have come to own.

Dear Mom and Dad,

These are the reasons why I don't want to cremate you when you die. These are the reasons why I want to bury you in a simple way.

First, bodies are sacred. We agree that life is fleeting—and I know that the older you become the more sensitive you become to this—but it is exactly because life is fleeting that our bodies are sacred. What you do with your body is much of what you leave here when you die. Our actions are sacred—or, have the potential to be sacred—as much as our meditations and prayers are. Too often, I think, we assume that what we do "in our heads" is more valuable than what we do in our bodies. What you do with your body is what you know to be true.

Mom, when you take the hand of the old woman at the soup kitchen, and Dad, when you sing out strong your love for God, you are showing your bodies to be sacred places. Can you see, then, why your physical body remains meaningful to me after you are done with it—why I would like to at least show it respect as one might a holy book (by burying it)? You created a lot of meaning in there.

Medieval Christians were fanatical on this point. Holy relics of the saints were big business. Pilgrims would travel for months on foot to reach a cathedral or some other holy place where they could see, or even touch, one of the bones of the martyrs, or a drop of the Virgin Mary's blood, or some other piece of physical remembrance of someone's body. I don't want to keep your bones around so that I can see and touch them, but I can understand—and even admire—the emotion and passion of those medieval pilgrims for their saints.

I like to have icons around our apartment. I also like to have pictures of your parents and grandparents around. I keep many books around, too—books that, in many cases, I may not read in detail again. But I like to be around people like Kierkegaard, Teresa of Avila, Dostoevsky, and Flannery O'Connor. Who wouldn't? The people behind our images are reminders of who we want to be. After you are gone, I want to be around you when I can. I want to be reminded—not of who you were—but of who you are—because our lives here are fleeting, and like a work of art, we live on in ways that we do not know or even understand.

Second, I want to plant your bodies like seeds. I've always found cemeteries fascinating. The bodies that are tucked in their coffins and placed snuggly in the ground there are planted as memories and foundations for what might come in the future. The New Testament says that the Lord will return and our bodies will be resurrected to meet him in the air. Fundamentalists interpret this passage literally. Medieval and Renaissance artists also depicted realistic pictures of body parts emerging from the mouths of beasts, raising from the ground and the waters, and reassembling in the air on the way to the clouds. I have no such visions. But after you die, I will see your body as a planting, like a new tree, to create new life—in the natural world and also in our family.

Third, I would like to let God be God. Even if we separate the soul from the body at death, your body remains the sacred vessel (not a "prison," as some mystics have said) for your soul here on earth. It was composed out of the earth, as we know from Genesis, and to the earth it should return. Cremation takes into our hands what the earth can easily and fruitfully accomplish on its own, in its time.

An elegant woman in her 80s recently told me this story about herself. She said: "I have a very good friend who died last year. She is about my age and we had been friends for decades. I know each of her nine children, and then their children. Most of her family still lives within easy driving distance of her home.

"The day that she died, her children gathered together in her home. They were not just sad, grieving. They washed her body." At this, the woman telling me the story began to cry.

"Her nine children encircled her body and washed it, lovingly. They told stories about their mother and they laughed and they cried. Then, someone called the funeral home and the hearse came to pick her up. The children, some of them in their sixties, carried their mother to the car and as it drove away to the funeral home, they stood in the street and waved."

Somewhere, William Blake said that dying was simply like passing from one room to the next. Blake died in his bed, singing, his biographers say. I believe that death is like that, too. And when it happens to you, I think you will soon find yourself in song.

Please don't worry about the mess you leave behind. I would like to be bothered with tending to it.

I wanted to give a gift of fundamentalism back to my parents. Danelle's serious illness regenerated our marriage and brought God into the center of it. Danelle's recovery was a new birth and a fresh chance to start over again. The eventual death of my parents will offer our family the same opportunity. Fundamentalism taught me the certainty of God's presence in our hearts and lives. There is nothing to be afraid of, in the dying, in the afterwards, or in what is left behind. Each death is a new life, like walking from one room to the next. My letter was one small piece of practicing the resurrection that not only is to come, but is here and now.

■ ■ ■ ■ ■ ■ ■ afterword

Who fails to cast his eye on the sun when it rises?
Who takes his eye off a comet when it breaks out?
Who doesn't bend his ear to any bell
     that has occasion to ring?
But, who can remove it from that bell which is
     passing a piece of himself out of this world?
—John Donne

Over the years, I've asked many friends a simple, seemingly obvious, question: "Why do we become parents? Why bother? What are the benefits?" It is remarkable how difficult it can be to answer that question.

I don't have in mind the tax breaks of parenthood. I mean: What makes us do it? The fear of not having anyone to whom we may pass on our legacy? The desire to satisfy our own parents' need to become grandparents? Some sort of narcissism, or self-love? I want to know, in order to satisfy my own confusion: Why do we bother to become parents when by doing it we only open ourselves up to pain?

Try it sometime. The question makes for a thoughtful conversation. Now, of course, I'm going to tell you what I think, but first, let me tell you my symptoms. I never really knew how to love with anything approaching godly love until I became a father. I felt pain from the moment that Danelle and I glimpsed the daughter that we created. It was as if my heart was broken open; I was vulnerable and ready to sacrifice everything for that new life.

In the end, the only answer to my own question that satisfies me is that real love eventually bursts out. God's love in us can do that, and human love simply, inevitably, sometimes mistakenly, results in children. That's just what love does. It creates. But it also sacrifices, and pains.

Danelle and I never intended for her to get pregnant, at least not when it happened. I've always marveled at those couples who describe how they precisely managed their lives down to the details of planning in which month they would like to give birth. A friend recently said to me: "My wife and I have decided that we need to first get our graduate school loans under control, then she wants to get her practice off the ground, and then we want to build on a guest room to the house—because, you know, it is quite small as it is—and then, we plan to start having kids." Danelle and I never had the opportunity to think that way.

Pregnancy was the last thing that her body needed after the unknown virus and long hospital stays. We wondered for years after her unfinished diagnosis if the symptoms would return, and when Danelle missed her period for the first time we felt only dread. It was only eleven weeks after she was finally dismissed from the hospital, and only eight weeks since her symptoms had faded away.

Fundamentalism has taught me nothing if not the reality that we are all of us born again and again. One life passes into another and it is all suspended in the eternity that we call time, in the timelessness that is our journey with God.

Danelle was pregnant. What a word! *We* were pregnant.

It was almost exactly a year to the day that Danelle was discharged from the hospital for the last time that our daughter, Sarah-Maria, was born. My heart was rent in two when she emerged from Danelle's womb. I was standing beside her and almost literally caught Sarah in my arms, as she screamed for life. The love that Danelle and I shared, and the pain that we experienced in such a short time, was culminated in the joy of that new life. It was a new birth for the three of us.

How could something so beautiful emerge from a situation that was so ugly, so painful? Here was a mess in our hands, a new organism of love, of God.

■ ■ ■ ■ ■ ■ ■ acknowledgments

The author wishes to thank the many readers of
www.explorefaith.org who read earlier drafts of several
of these chapters. Also, many thanks go to Pamela
Johnson, Robert Klausmeier, Lil Copan, Danelle
Sweeney, and Sharon Sims, all of whom offered
thoughtful and sensitive ears and eyes to the second
draft.

■ ■ ■ ■ ■ ■ ■ notes

introduction

p. ix *Somewhere in the Zohar it says. . .* Thanks to Rabbi Lawrence Kushner for calling my attention to this reference and its context.

one

p. 6 *. . . lent him to the LORD* 1 Samuel 1:28

p. 6 *I will give him unto the LORD . . .* 1 Samuel 1:11

p. 7 *Here am I. . . Go lie down . . .* 1 Samuel 3:8-9

two

p. 19 *He telleth the movement of the stars, . . .* Psalm 147:4-5

p. 22 *Thy words were found . . .* Jeremiah 15:16b

p. 23 *. . . confess with your mouth.* Romans 10:9a

p. 25 *Then shall he also say . . .* Matthew 25:41

three

p. 36 *Mr. Moody . . . rose to his feet . . .* From Harry Ironside, *Random Reminiscences from Fifty Years of Ministry* (Neptune, NJ: Loizeaux Brothers, 1939).

four

p. 42 *I am going to ask you to come* . . . (Billy Graham quote). From Richard Wightman Fox, *Jesus in America: Personal Savior, Cultural Hero, National Obsession* (HarperSanFrancisco, 2004), 352-353.

    p. 45 *Wherefore I say unto you* . . . Matthew 12:31-32

    p. 45 *And whosoever shall speak* . . . Luke 12:10

    p. 48 *One of the most poignant scenes in literature* . . . Thanks to Paul L. Holmer for calling my attention to this reference and its context. Professor Holmer died on June 29, 2004, and will be sorely missed by those of us who learned so much from him.

five

p. 50 *Everything is connected to everything else* . . . From Lawrence Kushner, *Invisible Lines of Connection* (Woodstock, VT: Jewish Lights Publishing, 1996).

    p. 54 *the world is crucified unto me* . . . Galatians 6:14

    p. 57 *When thou prayest* . . . Matthew 6:6

six

p. 65 *If therefore thou shalt not watch* . . . Revelation 3:3

seven

    p. 72 *the assurance of things hoped for,* . . . Hebrews 11:1

    p. 72 cf. Matthew 10:8, Acts 2:4, Acts 2:17

    p. 73 *put[ting] on the whole armor of God* . . . Ephesians 6:11a

nine

p. 92 *Go ye therefore, and teach* . . . Matthew 28:20

ten

p. 97   *Not to win souls . . .*   From John R. Rice, *The Ruin of a Christian* (Murfreesboro, TN: Sword of the Lord Publishing, 1944).

p. 98   *Thy kingdom come, thy will be done . . .*   Matthew 6:6

p. 98   *For whosoever shall do the will . . .*   Matthew 12:50

p. 98   *It is not the will of your Father . . .*   Matthew 18:14

p. 98   *Father. if thou be willing . . .*   Matthew 22:44

p. 98   *Jesus saith unto him . . .*   John 4:34

thirteen

p. 139   *My beloved is mine . . .*   Song of Solomon 2:16

p. 139   *Thou hast ravished my heart . . .*   Song of Solomon 4:9–10a

fourteen

p. 146   *Think not that I have come . . .*   Matthew 5:17

p. 146   *For I say unto you . . .*   Matthew 5:20

p. 147   *How amiable are thy tabernacles . . .*   Psalm 84:1-2, 8, 10

About Paraclete Press

Who We Are

Paraclete Press is an ecumenical publisher of books on Christian spirituality for people of all denominations and backgrounds.

We publish books that represent the wide spectrum of Christian belief and practice—Catholic, Orthodox and Protestant.

We market our books primarily through booksellers; we are what is called a "trade" publisher, which means that we like it best when readers buy our books from booksellers, our partners in successfully reaching as wide of an audience as possible.

We are uniquely positioned in the marketplace without connection to a large corporation or conglomerate and with informal relationships to many branches and denominations of faith, rather than a formal relationship to any single one. We focus on publishing a diversity of thoughts and perspectives—the fruit of our diversity as a company.

What We Are Doing

Paraclete Press is publishing books that show the diversity and depth of what it means to be Christian. We publish books that reflect the Christian experience across many cultures, time periods, and houses of worship.

We publish books about spiritual practice, history, ideas, customs, and rituals, and books that nourish the vibrant life of the church.

We have several different series of books within Paraclete Press, including the bestselling Living Library series of modernized classic texts, A Voice from the Monastery—giving voice to men and women monastics on what it means to live a spiritual life today, and Many Mansions—for exploring the riches of the world's religious traditions and discovering how other faiths inform Christian thought and practice.

Learn more about us at our website:
www.paracletepress.com, or call us toll-free at
1-800-451-5006.

Also by Jon M. Sweeney:

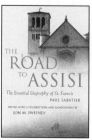

The Road to Assisi:
The Essential Biography of St. Francis
Paul Sabatier
Edited with Introduction and Annotations
by Jon M. Sweeney
187 pages
ISBN: 1-55725-401-X
$12.95, Trade Paper

A Selection of
Book of the Month Club • History Book Club
Crossings Book Club • The Literary Guild

In his 1894 biography of St. Francis, Paul Sabatier portrays a fully human Francis, with insecurities and fear, but also a gentle mystic and passionate reformer. This modern edition includes helpful sidebar explanatory notes, and is supplemented with the insights of scholars and writers, from Dante to Umberto Eco.

"Essential reading for anyone interested in the life and times of the great charismatic of Assisi. . . highly recommended."
—Valerie Martin, author of *Salvation: Scenes from the Life of St. Francis*

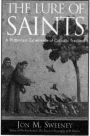

The Lure of Saints:
A Protestant Experience of Catholic Tradition
Jon M. Sweeney
237 pages
ISBN: 1-55725-419-2
$21.95, Hardcover

This compelling guide includes profiles of ancient, medieval and modern figures, East and West, the sublime and the unusual, with special chapters exploring:

• Differences between Catholic and Protestant imaginations.
• How saints were made in the past and how they are today.
• Devotions and spiritual practices.
• The radical triumph of the Protestant idea.
• Miracles, doubt, and belief.
• Tears, pain, foolishness, apparitions, stigmatas, and more strange, saintly behavior.

"A satisfying blend of the concrete (prayers, a list of feast days, 10 steps to living like asaint) with Sweeney's personal observations and historical information."—*Publishers Weekly*

Available from most booksellers or through Paraclete Press:
www.paracletepress.com • 1-800-451-5006.
Try your local bookstore first.